Language and Process

Intersections in Continental and Analytic Philosophy

Series Editors
Jeffrey A. Bell, Paul Livingston and James Williams

Drawing on different traditions for new solutions to philosophical problems

Books in this series will bring together work in the analytic and continental traditions in philosophy. Although these traditions have until recently been thought of as separate, if not irreconcilable, these books will show how key philosophical problems can be addressed by drawing from work in both.

The intersections on display here will demonstrate the strength and vitality of a pluralist approach to philosophy, as well as its wide relevance to contemporary philosophical concerns.

Books available
Language and Process: Words, Whitehead and the World, Michael Halewood

Visit the Intersections website at edinburghuniversitypress.com/
series-intersections-in-continental-and-analytic-philosophy

Language and Process

Words, Whitehead and the World

Michael Halewood

EDINBURGH
University Press

Edinburgh University Press is one of the leading university presses
in the UK. We publish academic books and journals in our selected
subject areas across the humanities and social sciences, combining
cutting-edge scholarship with high editorial and production
values to produce academic works of lasting importance. For more
information visit our website: edinburghuniversitypress.com

Edinburgh University Press Ltd
The Tun – Holyrood Road, 12(2f) Jackson's Entry, Edinburgh EH8 8PJ

First published in hardback by Edinburgh University Press 2020

Typeset in Bembo
by R. J. Footring Ltd, Derby

A CIP record for this book is available from the British Library

ISBN 978 1 4744 4910 6 (hardback)
ISBN 978 1 4744 4911 3 (paperback)
ISBN 978 1 4744 4912 0 (webready PDF)
ISBN 978 1 4744 4913 7 (epub)

Contents

Acknowledgements vi

Preface viii

1 Introduction: The Problem of Words *and* Things 1

2 Nouns, Names and Signs: From Frege to Saussure 15

3 Adjectives: The Properties of the World and the
'Bifurcation of Nature' 34

4 Verbs: Deleuze on Infinitives, Events and Process 51

5 Adverbs: Dewey on the Qualities of Existence 71

6 Prepositions: Whitehead on the 'Withness' of the Body 89

7 Gender and Personal Pronouns: She, He, It and They 110

8 Tone, Force and Rhetoric: Capitalism, Theology
and Grammar 135

9 Conclusion 154

Bibliography 158

Index 163

Acknowledgements

I would like to thank the series editors, Jeff Bell, Paul Livingston and James Williams, for their encouragement and support. Carol Macdonald and Kirsty Woods at Edinburgh University Press have provided patient and invaluable help and guidance.

There are two people who in their very special and different ways have provided the real reason for writing this book: thank you, Vanessa; and welcome, Leo.

'Rose is a rose is a rose' – Gertrude Stein

Preface

Although rarely made explicit, there are two predominant approaches to understanding the relationship between language and the world. One position holds that there are things in the world, and that words act as names for these things. These names, it is supposed, stand in for, grasp on to, or capture the things of the world. This is reflected in the way that some people try to teach language to children: 'This *is* a ball, a cat, a dog' – and they have pictures to back up their statements. Language is regarded as having a direct and fixed relation to the things of the world.

The second main approach is succinctly expressed in a line from Shakespeare: 'that which we call a rose by any other name would smell as sweet'. Taken at face value, this line suggests that there are things in the world, such as roses, that have their own properties, such as smelling sweet. The words that we use to describe them, the names that we give them, may change or vary but the properties of these things will stay the same. In this sense, words do not map directly on to the world; they are just human artifices that are unable to fully capture the world. As the songwriter Paddy McAloon once put it: 'Words are trains for moving past what really has no name.'

Both of these approaches have some force. Yet they also carry a range of problems. If words are taken as capturing the world, or indicating how the world *is*, the question arises of those words that can have different meanings on different occasions, thus appearing to pick out different items. It becomes difficult to maintain that words name things directly when one of the joys of language is that different words can be used to refer to the same thing. Cats and dogs are both animals and pets; a ball could be called a sphere or an orb. Moreover, one word can refer to two completely different things: a ball could be a dance. The second approach escapes such problems by emphasising the contingency of the meanings of words, and the lack of fixity in the relation of language to the world. But it does so at a price. Do we really want to say that the word 'atom' does not describe something that is real? Does the word 'green' only relate to my private experience of the world – do other people see 'green' in the same way? If language does not put us in direct contact with the world, then the implication is that the world itself is mute and dislocated from us and our language.

In the course of this book, I will outline some of the theoretical arguments and presumptions that lie behind these two approaches, arguing that both positions are inadequate in accounting for the relation between words and things. Treating language as a way of naming the things of the world leads to the problem of reaching across the gap between things and the words that are used to name such things. Insisting that words are only human creations produces another gap, so that words say more about us than about the world. What is required is a reconsideration of the ideas, problems and concepts that led to these questions being formulated in such a way. The overall aim of this book is not to disprove or correct previous theories but to consider what problems they were addressing and to reorient how these are envisaged. In doing so it aims to provide new and productive ways of thinking about a range of topics and concepts.

The chapters that follow will use examples from philosophy, science, social theory, feminism, linguistics, poetry and so on, as and when the arguments or topics require. Within the modern division of academic labour, researchers in one field often have little knowledge of, or interest in, developments in other fields. This is certainly the case for analyses of language (and its relation to the world) where linguistics, philosophy, sociology, anthropology, cultural studies etc. have tended to go their own ways.

One guiding thread that runs throughout the book is the work of Alfred North Whitehead (1861–1947), whose ideas are becoming increasingly important for current debates. This is certainly the case with regard to the apparent problems involved in understanding the relations between language and the world. On the one hand, Whitehead's work provides an incisive critique of the conceptual presumptions and presuppositions that linger within many theories of both language and of the world. On the other, his work offers a way of reapproaching and reorienting our thought and our questions, so as to avoid such presumptions. As will be seen, along with John Dewey, Gilles Deleuze, Luce Irigaray and others, Whitehead invites us to concentrate on the processes that inhere in both the world and language.

1

Introduction:
The Problem of Words *and* Things

During the twentieth century, the analysis of language became a central concern within many fields of academic study. This is often referred to as the 'linguistic turn' and can be found in diverse arenas such as analytic philosophy, sociology, social theory, anthropology, cultural studies, social psychology and beyond. Although it may not be possible to isolate one factor that explains both how and why analyses of language became so predominant, it is, perhaps, possible to identify a common theme, a shared problem, which runs through these disparate disciplines. This is to do with the relationship of words and things, of language and the world.

The relation between words and things is not as straightforward as might first appear. One reason for this, as Alfred North Whitehead once remarked, is that 'the little word "and" is a nest of ambiguity' (Whitehead 1938: 74). The word 'and' normally operates as a conjunction, in that it links different terms. Yet the character of such links varies widely. It can indicate opposites, suggest a good pairing, or demarcate a contrast (for example, 'black and white', 'fish and chips', 'salt and pepper', respectively). In recent years, a movement within philosophy under the umbrella term 'Speculative Realism' has highlighted the specific ambiguity involved in phrases such as 'words *and* things', 'language *and* the world'. Speculative Realism is a term coined in 2007 by Alberto Toscano when he was organising a conference at Goldsmiths, University of London, and needed a title for the event. The phrase was chosen to indicate the shared interests of the diverse thinkers who had agreed to attend: Ray Brassier, Iain Hamilton Grant, Graham Harman and Quentin Meillassoux. Although it is not easy to provide a definition, and these writers have subsequently gone their own philosophical ways,[1] it is possible to outline the starting point upon which they would all agree. This is to be found in the critical position developed by Quentin Meillassoux in his book *After Finitude* (2008).

Meillassoux argues that both science and philosophy, although in different ways, lay claim to knowledge of, for example, a tree, as it objectively exists 'out there' in the world. This knowledge, however, has only been gained through the activity of thinking about that tree. Such thoughts mediate and constitute the mind's relation to the tree, making it impossible to jump out of such thoughts and get directly to the tree in itself, as it is separately from such thoughts, from the mind. According to Meillassoux, this makes it impossible to know what the tree is 'in itself', as knowledge of that tree is always tied to a thinking of the tree, to how the tree appears for us, for human knowledge or consciousness.

This constitutes a major paradox that lurks behind modern thought, which Meillassoux calls 'correlationism' or 'the correlationist circle'. He provides the following definition: it is 'the idea according to which we only ever have access to the correlation between thinking and being, and never to either term considered apart from the other' (Meillassoux 2008: 5). Correlationism is a legacy of the philosophy of Kant (or a widespread understanding of the philosophy of Kant). One of Kant's innovations was to argue that the mind does not act as some kind of mirror or receptacle of the external world. Rather, as another speculative realist, Levi Bryant, puts it, according to Kant, 'the mind does not merely reflect reality, but rather *actively structures* reality'

---

1. As with all schools of thought, there have been disagreements and splits. Indeed, Graham Harman has since commented that Speculative Realism only lasted for that one day at Goldsmiths, and Harman has now developed what he calls Object-Oriented-Ontology (OOO), which he attempts to distinguish from 'traditional' Speculative Realism.

(Bryant 2015: 46, emphasis in original). Kant also differentiated between things-in-themselves (noumena) and the appearance of such things to human cognition (phenomena). Within this philosophical model, human experience and thinking cannot access these things-in-themselves, noumena, as they are always tied to the activity of thinking which mediates, or even constitutes, the mind's relation with such things. As a result, things-in-themselves become unknowable in themselves; their separate existence from the mind is never directly accessible to the mind. Acquaintance with them, or knowledge of them, is only possible in terms of their appearance or manifestation *to* human minds.[2] This leaves an unknown remainder, forever ungraspable, which constitutes the secret lives of other entities, things or beings. There is, on one side, the world in itself and, on the other, human understanding of the world.

It is important to note that Meillassoux is not some postmodernist or extreme sceptic who wants to undermine the possibility of science. He is clear that the correlationist situation is untenable; it needs to be overcome. Correlationism is 'an indefensible thesis because thought cannot get *outside itself* in order to compare the world as it is "in itself" to the world "as it is for us"' (Meillassoux 2008: 3, emphasis in original). Furthermore, although Meillassoux's argument is presented at the level of the correlation of thought and being, its reach extends to other areas. For example, in so far as thought is tied to consciousness, and consciousness is linked to language, then the correlationist circle would also seem to apply to the relation between language and the world, as will be discussed throughout this chapter.

How Many Words for Snow?

It is sometimes claimed that 'Eskimos' have as many as fifty words to describe varieties of snow. I have put inverted commas around

---

2. The importance of this little word 'to', acting as a preposition, will be taken up in Chapter 6.

the word 'Eskimos' for a reason. This lumping together of vastly different humans under one name comes from a lack of awareness of the diversity of the groups and individuals that it is supposed to indicate (see Samson 2003 for more on this important topic). This is one first indication of the problem of naming which will be taken up in the next chapter, and of questions of language and power which will be taken up in Chapters 7 and 8.

Taking this example at face-value, for the moment at least, it is supposed that 'Eskimos' have a wide range of terms to describe, for example, 'snow that has just fallen', 'snow that has thawed and refrozen', 'snow that is unstable', and so on. 'Eskimos' live in an environment where snow and ice play an important part, so a wide range of words for snow is required to be able to live. This implies that 'Eskimos' see the world differently and this is reflected in their language; there is a link between language, thinking and understanding the world. The greater number of words for snow points to the fact that they live in a very different world from 'us'. This is an example of the Sapir–Whorf hypothesis[3] which relies on two related ideas: 'linguistic relativity' and 'linguistic determinism'. Both of these ideas fall prey to the correlationist paradox as they prioritise language as the vehicle for understanding the world, making it impossible to access the world in itself without the mediation of a specific language.

Linguistic relativity is the 'belief that each language embodies and perpetuates a particular world view' (Brown 1968: 230). This suggests that the members of a society or a country who speak a common language share both a language and a specific way of viewing and understanding 'reality'. 'The speakers of a language are partners to an agreement to perceive and think of the world in a certain way' (Brown 1968: 230). Linguistic determinism makes a related but even stronger claim. It asserts that,

---

3. This term comes from the merging of the names of two pioneers of linguistics, Benjamin Lee Whorf (1897–1941) and his mentor, Edward Sapir (1884–1939).

in addition to the link between a given language and a particular way of seeing the world, how we think of the world is *determined* by the language that we use. So: 'The languages of the world are so many molds of varying shape into which infant minds are poured' (Brown 1968: 231).

The Sapir–Whorf hypothesis is another example of Meillassoux's notion of correlationism. Any use of human language expresses human thoughts about the world. This creates a vicious circle where language and thinking always get in the way of directly accessing the world as it is, separate from talking or thinking about it. Each language constitutes a specific rendering of a specific 'reality', rather than an accurate or objective picture of the world. We are condemned to remain within the realm of our language, only vaguely pointing to an outside world which forever evades our linguistic grasp. 'We' (humans with language) seem to have lost any innocent contact with the other side, with the world, as our language always acts as an intermediary. There is the world and there is language. The two sit on different sides of an unbridgeable gulf, or so it seems. And, as Whitehead puts it: 'The worst of a gulf is, that it is very difficult to know what is happening on the further side of it' (Whitehead 1933: 217).

Before moving on, it is worth noting two problems with the Sapir–Whorf hypothesis. When outlining the 'Eskimo' example, the following phrase was used: 'they live in a very different world from "us"'. This raises the question of who is included in this 'us'. It may have been that the original aim of (linguistic) anthropologists such as Sapir and Whorf was to indicate the richness of 'Eskimo' culture and to point out that it is certainly equal, indeed in some ways superior, to that of the West. But this runs the risk of making 'Eskimo' more exotic or quaint, in its very distinctiveness, when compared with the more humdrum character of Western languages and the kind of thought or mind-set which is associated with such languages. It also involves playing down the differences between individual European languages, tacitly creating a 'Western outlook', while assigning completely different 'realities' or world-views to speakers of 'Eskimo' or to indigenous groups in the Amazon rainforest, for example. In turn, this implies that this Western outlook sets an unwarranted benchmark against which other world-views are judged. The small word 'us' is not as innocent or as straightforward as might first appear and, as is the case with other words, it should be treated with caution.

There is another major problem with the Sapir–Whorf hypothesis, as set out in the 'Eskimo' example. It assumes that single words are the main way of indicating the things of the world. If there are three different words for snow in 'Eskimo' which do not directly map on to three different words in English, then those who speak 'Eskimo' must think of snow and the world differently. This overlooks that speakers of English, especially those who make snowballs, are often aware of different kinds of snow but use phrases rather than individual words to describe these; examples of such phrases might be 'good snow for packing', 'bad snow for packing'. English-speakers may not have as many individual words for snow as 'Eskimos' are imagined to have, but there are an equivalent number of possible phrases for snow. The problem of maintaining that individual words, or phrases, somehow map on to individual items in the world will be taken up in the next chapter after a further discussion of correlationism and the concept of 'reality'.

A Problem with Reality?

One of the strengths of Speculative Realism is that it highlights the extent to which correlationism has infected contemporary conceptions of language, thinking and the world. The speculative realists may have been correct in their diagnosis but the next step is more difficult. How do we escape this problem? Is it possible to jump out of our language, or our thought, and gain immediate access to the world as it is, to the 'great outdoors', as Meillassoux calls it (2008: 7)? Meillassoux maintains that it is possible to use thought as the weapon with which we can make our escape, by turning thought back on itself, and forcing it to recognise the necessity of contingency (Meillassoux 2008: 74–80). Graham Harman, another, though former, speculative realist, takes a different approach. Harman insists that the things of the world should not be treated as irreducibly separate and different from humans: the things of the world have their own 'lives' and are not merely food for our knowledge of the world. Granting some kind of life to things (to 'objects') means that they should be viewed as actors in the world with their own concerns. These lives are constituted by the numerous relations in which such things engage (although they are not completely explainable by, or reducible to, such relations). In this way, Harman maintains that it is possible to outline a 'realism of autonomous things without matter' (Harman 2009: 132). He also states that 'Material bodies cannot possibly do justice to the reality of things in themselves' (Harman 2009: 143). Later chapters will provide a fuller account of the importance of establishing new ways of thinking which do not treat humans as exceptions, and which enable the things of the world to have lives of their own. However, Harman's mention of the 'reality of things in themselves' raises a more immediate problem.

According to the tacit acceptance of the correlationist circle, as discussed above, direct access to the world appears impossible without thought or language intervening, thereby polluting the purity of the reality of 'things in themselves'. It seems that 'reality-as-it-is' has become impossible to grasp or name. All that remains is our *concept* of reality. If reality is only a concept rather than a genuine state of affairs, then we are stranded on one side of a gulf, the human side. We are again isolated in the realm of language and concepts, set adrift from the world-as-it-is. Words cannot latch on to the world. This position risks following the strongest version of the Sapir–Whorf hypothesis. Language constructs our reality. We are prisoners of our words and thoughts. Each culture produces its own reality through its own language. This could be pushed further. In so far as all individuals have their own vocabularies, ways of phrasing sentences, of speaking, each individual human has their own 'private' language. This would also suggest that each individual has their own private reality. The initial problem of language and the world has quickly led to solipsism. Other people and the world become figments of the imagination. We are utterly alone with only our *concept* of reality for solace.

Can this problem of reality be avoided? As will be argued throughout this book, it is not possible, or even worthwhile, to try and bridge any supposed gap between our apparently private thoughts, our language and the world ('reality'), as it is the very presumption of such a gap that constitutes the main problem. Following Whitehead, it is better to trace how this position, this problem, was constituted and to develop avenues of thought that enable this impasse to be avoided or sidestepped. For example, Chapter 5 will offer a very different approach to such questions, in terms of process and adverbs, through a sustained analysis of the work of John Dewey (1859–1942). Dewey argues that if a strict division is made between the world and experience of the world, then 'psycho-physical and mental functions became in-explicable anomalies, supernatural in the literal sense of the word' (Dewey 1958: 265). Dewey indicates that the idea of a private mental realm only comes about *after* the formulation of the idea of a fixed reality that is 'out there' and that makes up the external world. It is in this sense 'supernatural', as it arises out of the prior premising of a *concept* of reality, supposedly comprised of a 'natural order of things'. It is only once a conception of this natural order of things has been established that it is possible to compare such a conception of reality to that other realm which constitutes human thought, language and experience; a realm which, by comparison, is not so natural, so real, so susceptible to universal laws of nature. This is the realm of the supernatural in the literal sense that it is 'above' or 'beyond' nature. This 'subjective' realm of our individual thoughts and words is only dislocated from a very specific concept of reality. And, as Durkheim reminds us, this idea 'is of recent origin'. Perhaps 'reality' is not as real as is sometimes thought:

In order to say that certain things are supernatural, it is necessary to have the sentiment that a *natural order of things* exists, that is to say, that the phenomena of the universe are bound together by necessary connections, called laws [. . .] But this idea of universal determinism is of recent origin. (Durkheim 2008: 26, emphasis in original)

The concept of reality came to be at a certain point in time. As a result, the gap between the world and human experience, between thought and reality, between words and things, is not in itself 'real' or 'natural'. There is a need to pay attention to how concepts are constructed, and not to become so immersed in the problems that they appear to produce that it is forgotten that they have a history. A recognition of this history will allow for a recognition of the different routes that could have be taken to avoid such problems. Later chapters will offer such alternative routes, such as that of process, through an analysis of writers such as Whitehead, Deleuze, Dewey, Irigaray and Marx.

Looking Forward

The previous discussion has been mostly critical, in that it has set out a range of problems to do with language, the world and reality. A more positive approach, which will be developed in later chapters, is to argue that if our concept of reality came to be, gained its 'reality', at a certain point, then this allows the problem of correlationism to be rethought. This is not to suggest that our concept of reality is imaginary. That would be to fall into the correlationist trap, as it would assume that our concept of reality was supernatural, in that it does not correspond to a more fundamental reality (which itself has not yet been defined or identified). It is hard to shake off the claims of the concept of reality. As a result, in the chapters that follow, the word 'reality' will be used only when summarising or describing the points of view of other writers. Instead, I have made extensive use of the term 'world' without making any strong commitment to a clearly defined standpoint or definition. The use of this term does not imply any theory of the world and is not intended as a replacement for the word 'reality'. The term 'world' helps to establish a locale from which a range of arguments will develop. While some might prefer the term 'worlds', in order not to prescribe any limits at too early a stage and to indicate an openness to a range of possibilities, I have retained the singular form, because, as will be seen in the chapters that follow, both the world and language hold more potential than is sometimes thought.

To avoid the vicious circle, where language seems to make us its prisoner, where it is impossible to talk or think about the outside world in itself, one important first step is not to make any assumptions about either language or the world. Not making an assumption might seem to be a rather tepid starting point. However, it could also be seen as a decisive move. Whitehead makes a clear link between humility, boldness and speculation: 'Speculative boldness must be balanced by complete humility before logic, and before fact. It is a disease of philosophy when it is neither bold nor humble, but merely a reflection of the temperamental presuppositions of exceptional personalities' (Whitehead 1978: 17). This book will try to follow Whitehead's advice by starting out from the seemingly innocent (even humble) position that language is itself a part of the world. There is no gap between language and the world. The speculative boldness appears when this leads to the realisation that words are as much a part of the world as things are. Indeed, words are probably another kind of thing. This is not to reduce words or language to some kind of static fact. The world is made up of a vast array of different things, all of which have different roles and potentials, from elephants to emails, quarks to quinine, soldiers to soldering irons. Words and language need to be given their rightful place within this array. The 'answer' is not to prioritise one aspect, either language or the world, thinking or being, but to develop alternative approaches which are able to incorporate both elements.

It should be noted that although the argument set out so far has relied heavily on the concept of correlationism and some of the ideas of Harman and Meillassoux, this book is not about Speculative Realism. As Debaise (2017: 12–15) has discussed, there are similarities between the diagnoses made by speculative realists with regard to correlationism and Whitehead's outline of the problem of the bifurcation of nature (which will be discussed further in Chapter 3). Shaviro (2014) has also provided a sustained analysis of the similarities and differences between Speculative Realism and the work of Whitehead. There are certainly resonances between Whitehead and Speculative Realism, and this book *could* be read only as an engagement with the problem of correlationism, through the specific concerns of the relation of language and the world, of words and things. However, this would risk setting up correlationism as the only problem, or the only way of setting out the problem. It would also, tacitly perhaps, suggest that there is one solution that would respond to all aspects of this problem. The problem of correlationism is a very specific one which provides an insight into a particular set of questions to do with thinking and the world. Correlationism is only one example, among many, of what Whitehead calls 'bifurcation'.

The aim is not to solve the problem of correlationism or the 'problem of language'; it is to avoid them, by offering different routes. It is possible to accept the critical force of the problem of correlationism as set out by Speculative Realism without accepting it as the only problem, the most immediate one, which has to be resolved in order to provide a better, more complete concept of reality. Following Whitehead, the aim is to broaden the remit of the problem of the relation of language and the world. This will involve a widening of what constitutes human experience and thought. 'The main sources of evidence respecting this width of human experience are language, social institutions, and action, including the fusion of the three which is language interpreting action and social institutions' (Whitehead 1933: 291). Furthermore, and as discussed previously, the concept of reality is itself a problem, but this does not mean that a better concept of reality is required. There is a need to ask

11

how and why this concept of reality has become so central, and to become aware of how it limits our thought, and blocks off new avenues of thought, by placing us within a well-rehearsed set of questions (and responses). It is important to consider why it is felt that an overarching concept of reality is needed at all. Whitehead only uses the word 'reality' 33 times in the 351 pages of *Process and Reality*. He is much more concerned with actuality than with any concept of reality. Rather than trying to account for the manner of existence of *every* thing in the universe, in existence, which would be to remain within an old-fashioned notion of reality, it is better to rid ourselves of the desire to talk about all things, at once and in abstract. Yet there is also a genuine need for speculative thought.

Whitehead (1978) and one of his key interpreters, Isabelle Stengers (2011; 2014), both indicate that the role of speculative thought is to produce new ways of thinking and approaching a range of problems, questions, assumptions and histories. It is not about trying to provide a description of all reality. This is a mistake that is often made by commentators on Whitehead's own metaphysical treatise, *Process and Reality*. Whitehead is not trying to describe what the world is really like. By stating that reality is a process, Whitehead may well be encouraging us, enabling us, to think in terms of process, but this does not imply that 'all is process'. This is too easy an answer. Whitehead is offering us some specific ways out of specific problems. Most especially, he is trying to resist a temptation that runs through much of our modern culture of thought, namely, to bifurcate the world into irreconcilable camps, such as the division between a supposedly utterly real factual world and human experiences, thoughts or statements about such a world. This book will use the relation of words and things as a focus, in order to bring certain problems to light and then to cast them in a different shade.

Whitehead's texts provide open, even revisable, concepts. This does not mean that they are not rigorous or coherent: it means that more is asked of us (remembering that this 'us' is not as clearly defined or as innocent as may first appear). His

12

ideas need to be rendered in terms of our own specific concerns and problems. In the chapters that follow, I have attempted to approach, from different angles, certain problems related to the question of words and things. Each chapter addresses a different problem and addresses a range of questions and considerations, such as: Can words capture the world? Can adverbs express the process of existence? What is the role of the body within language? What is gendered about language? How can we talk about capitalism? These do not build into a general theory about words and things. I do not see this as a limitation, as this approach stems from my understanding of the implications of Whitehead's metaphysics.[4] Whitehead is offering possible escape routes from certain philosophical problems, but these escape routes are for us to develop and investigate; they are not ready-made and do not constitute a better picture of the world (or 'reality'). Whitehead has given us signposts rather than a map.

The structure of the book is as follows: Chapters 2 and 3 will offer a critical analysis of a range of approaches to the relation of words and things, of language and the world, in terms of names (nouns), signs, descriptions (adjectives) and secondary qualities. In doing so, they will set out the main concerns of the book. The next three chapters will be more 'positive' as they suggest possible ways of reapproaching these questions, through the work of writers such as John Dewey, Gilles Deleuze and Alfred North Whitehead. This will involve an attempt to think language as part of the world, a world which is itself not a thing, but involves process. It will also involve a discussion of Whitehead's description of 'bodilyness', as expressed through prepositions, placing thought, language, the mind and the world in constant interrelation. Chapters 7 and 8 will use these insights to provide a fuller understanding of the complex intertwining of

---

4. I should make it clear that my understanding of Whitehead is deeply indebted to reading the texts of Isabelle Stengers, listening to her lectures and talks, as well as conversations with her over a number of years. I think that I have probably embedded more elements of her work in this book than I have made explicit.

words and things as they play out in terms of both gender and capitalism. The final chapter will revisit some of the implications of the book as a whole.

2

Nouns, Names and Signs: From Frege to Saussure

This chapter will outline how the development of two new academic fields in the late nineteenth and early twentieth centuries, namely, the philosophy of language and semiology, shifted focus away from theories that hold that specific words, 'nouns', simply name the objects of the world. What is of interest is the manner in which such moves were made and the avenues of analysis to which these arguments led. As will be seen, the view that language somehow immediately captures the world was one of the first casualties of the battle to establish the logical or scientific basis of language. This chapter traces the ways in which a range of authors brought the analysis of language to the fore and, correspondingly, how questions regarding the status or role of the world moved into the background. Only once these are established and understood will it be possible to recognise the force of the problems involved and to develop alternative routes that can think language and the world together.

Nouns and Names

The idea that there is a certain class of words that names the things of the world is a powerful and enduring one. However, developing a theory that explains or justifies such an approach is not as straightforward as it first appears. One major problem is the question of whether ordinary nouns (such as 'book' or 'lion') pick out or denote the things of the world in the same way that proper names, such as Barack Obama or Donald Trump, appear to pick out or denote real human individuals in the world. This is a question with a long history.

In the book of Genesis (2:19–20), it is reported that God gathered together all the animals of the world and, as the New King James version puts it, 'brought them to Adam to see what he would call them. And whatever Adam called each living creature, that was its name. So Adam gave names to all cattle, to the birds of the air, and to every beast of the field.'[1] There are (at least) two ways of reading this. It is clear that Adam names the animals, but the status of these names is unclear. Are they arbitrary? Could Adam have chosen any name for any animal, so that tigers could have been called lions and lions could have been called tigers? Such a view can be found in those modern approaches that treat words as conventions, so that each society, culture or language is able to decide upon its own words (for example, what is referred to as the boot of a car in the UK is termed the trunk in the US). There is another way of understanding this biblical quotation. Perhaps Adam's naming of the animals is the very moment when human language was created. However, this creation was not purely arbitrary. Adam had found the essential name of all the creatures; names that were already there, lying in wait to be dis-covered. What Adam did was uncover the true names of all the animals and bring them to light – 'that was its name' *and still is its name*. This implies that the various words that are currently used in different languages for the same animal (tigris, tigre, tygr, etc.) are simply translations of the one, true, original way of indicat-ing a tiger and that behind these different words lies the essence of tigerness, and it is this that is somehow being pointed to, or

---

1. Although not always to the fore in such debates, the question of power runs through this problem. Who has the authority to decide what things are called? It might be asked why it is Adam who chooses all the names, while Eve does not play any part. Is language 'man'-made, rather than 'human-made'? The question of power in relation to words and things, what it means to be named a man or woman, will be discussed in more detail in Chapter 7.

named, in various ways in the different languages of the world. Both readings assume that words act as names.[2]

In the late nineteenth and early twentieth centuries, such questions were reoriented and given a new impetus through investigations into the logical basis of language and the status of names and nouns. Three of the most important thinkers in this area were Gottlob Frege (1848–1925), Bertrand Russell (1872–1970) and Ludwig Wittgenstein (1889–1951).

Frege, Language and Logic

Frege's first concern was the philosophy of mathematics. His aim was to provide a foundation for the possibility of mathematical knowledge by establishing its logical basis. This, he believed, involved outlining a system through which mathematical inferences could be made. In turn, this required a systematic language that was capable of accurately expressing these inferences; one able to convey the logical structure of mathematical inferences through sentences that were themselves structured logically. Logical inconsistencies in language were not just minor irritations for Frege, as they were potential counter-examples that not only threatened the ability of language to match the inferences of mathematics but also presented significant problems for establishing the logical basis of mathematics. It is for this reason that a range of problems concerning how nouns operate, and whether they had the status of names, became a major concern for Frege.

If nouns operate as proper names appear to do, by simply picking out or denoting individuals in the world, then they fall prey to certain problems regarding proper names. The heart of the problem of whether nouns act as names involves questions regarding the (logical) status of those names or nouns that do

2. Plato's dialogue *Cratylus* is an early and important discussion of the problem of names, and it sets out the problems and advantages of thinking of names as either conventions or natural.

not denote an actual object, such as 'Excalibur' or 'phlogiston'. Likewise, nouns such as 'nobody' or 'anybody' do not have any direct referents, so how do they manage to convey meaning? Moreover, there are instances when different names seem to indicate the same entity.

Take, for example, the well-known but, as yet, unidentified street-artist, Bansky. The name Banksy refers to a person. If it is then discovered that this person's 'legal name' is Nick Hind, then the statement 'Nick Hind is Banksy' would be of great interest to many people. However, if a name (or noun) simply stands as a direct reference to an object (in this case a person), if its meaning simply comes from what it refers to, then the statement 'Bansky is Bansky' should have the same status as 'Nick Hind is Banksy'. The challenge is to establish where the extra 'meaning' comes from in the cases of different proper names that apparently refer to the same thing or person. Within Frege's logico-mathematical approach, the logical structure of the original statement, 'Nick Hind is Banksy', is 'A = B'. If A really is equivalent to B, then B can be substituted for A. For example, if 'A = 4' and 'B = $\sqrt{16}$', then A and B can used interchangeably. In the same way, if names operate by direct designation, then names that refer to the same entity should also be interchangeable. Hence 'Nick Hind is Banksy' should have the same meaning as 'Bansky is Bansky' or 'Nick Hind is Nick Hind'. Yet this is clearly not the case. The first statement seems to provide new information, but how? Although the full details of Frege's response to this question[3] are not crucial for the argument being set out here,

---

3. It should be noted that Frege established a difference between 'sense' and 'reference' (Frege 1980: 56ff.). In doing so, he was forced to posit new entities and new relations between these entities. For example: 'senses are objective and abstract entities' (Daly 2013: 23). And: 'a concept is not a mental entity. It is an abstract entity: it is neither mental nor physical. Moreover, a concept is a mind-independent entity. There may be concepts that no one ever thinks of just as there may be objects that no one ever thinks of' (Daly 2013: 39). As will be seen in the next section, Russell felt that the introduction of new entities, relations and distinctions by

Frege's attempt to resolve this issue through the insistence on the priority of the logical structure of sentences, rather than individual words or phrases, has implications that will be taken up throughout this book.

Frege maintains that, taken on their own, the component phrases within a sentence are not meaningful, as they are incomplete. Incomplete predicates or concepts[4] such as 'barks loudly', 'has four wheels', 'has a 60GB memory' do not pick out anything in the world, so they do not mean anything. Particular phrases (or predicates) need to be 'completed' by adding words such as 'the' or 'my' or 'this'. For example: 'the car that I am driving has four wheels', 'my dog barks loudly', 'this computer has a 60 GB memory'. It is only once a sentence is completed that its logical status can be ascertained, that it can be said to have any genuine meaning. Importantly, when a sentence is completed, according to Frege, it *does* act as if it were a proper name by directly picking out entities. This raises the question of what kind of entity is referred to in sentences. Frege's answer would be 'an object', but he has a very particular understanding of what constitutes an object: Frege 'introduces objects as the referents of proper names rather than introducing proper names as those expressions which refer to objects' (Daly 2013: 17). This is an inversion of the traditional approach in which the question is 'Given that there are objects in the world, how does language refer to or capture these objects?' Instead, Frege puts language first. He starts with a theory of predicates, sentences and proper names, focusing on

---

Frege was overly elaborate and ultimately went against the aim of a philosophy based on logic to be as succinct as possible and not to introduce new abstract concepts or entities if at all possible. As will be seen, Russell maintained that there was no need to make a distinction between 'sense' and 'reference', and that within Frege's 'theory of predication' there was enough material from which to establish a logico-mathematical scheme for the analysis of language.

4. In the following discussion, I will use the term 'concept' interchangeably with 'predicate'. Perhaps this is not strictly correct, for concepts, in Frege's work, are what are designated by predicates. But I believe that my usage makes Frege's argument clearer and is not incorrect.

the functions of these component parts within a more general system. Once the logical status of language has been established, he describes objects as those entities that are referred to by such proper names.[5] The world 'falls under' language rather than vice versa.

A further implication of Frege's position (one that influenced the development of analytic philosophy in the UK, USA, Australia and Scandinavia throughout the twentieth century) is that a sentence does not immediately refer to the world but to a thought about the world, to the 'thought-content' of a sentence. This thought-content is what is conveyed via language and is often referred to as a 'proposition'. The same proposition can be expressed in different sentences. For example: 'It is raining today in London' and 'Precipitation is currently falling in London.' Frege highlights the importance of getting beyond the immediate words and phraseology in a sentence to discover its logical structure in terms of the proposition, which concerns, for example, the possibility of getting wet if a person lives in London and ventures outside today. This focus on propositions is one of the most influential (and contentious) aspects of Frege's work and his influence on analytic philosophy in the twentieth century.

Frege has given priority to the logical status of language. As a result, when he does invoke the relationship of language to something beyond the immediate terms and relations in a sentence, it is to state that a sentence only has meaning when it is put in such a way that it can subsequently be judged to be true or false.

> We are therefore driven into accepting the *truth-value* of a sentence as constituting what it means . . . [every] sentence concerned with what its words mean is therefore to be regarded as a proper name, and its meaning, if it has one, is either the True or the False. (Frege 1980: 63)

---

5. These objects are not simple, material entities. By 'object' Frege 'does not mean *perceivable object*. He uses the term "proper name" to apply also to places, instants, periods of time and numbers' (Daly 2013: 17).

Frege retains one element of the model of language which holds that meaning is concerned with picking out, referring to or denoting things in the world, but he has radically altered the manner in which such referring or denoting takes place. It is now concerned with specific kinds of sentences (propositions) which gain their meaning only in so far as they can be judged to be either true or false. Sentences do not immediately refer to the world; they act as proper names which refer to truth-values (whether the sentence is true or false) and not to the world itself. It is in this sense that Frege's theory is sometimes referred to as resembling a form of Platonism (see, for example, Daly 2013: 18), and it set the path for subsequent analyses of language such as those developed by Bertrand Russell in which 'the world' has a secondary status when compared with the importance of establishing the logical consistency of propositions and statements.

Russell and the 'Theory of Descriptions'

Although not widely published or read in his own lifetime, Frege's ideas were taken up by Russell, who accepted Frege's argument for the need to establish the truth or falsehood of language statements, in terms of propositions. Like Frege, Russell was concerned with how a valid account of the status of nouns and names could be developed. Russell agreed with Frege in his contention that all sentences share a logical form that may be masked by its grammatical form, and that logico-mathematical notation[6] was the tool to uncover such forms (although Russell ultimately ended Frege's career by pointing out a paradox in one of his statements about the founding of mathematics).[7]

---

6. Russell worked with Alfred North Whitehead to systematise such mathematical notation in their monumental work *Principia Mathematica*.

7. Russell's paradox is concerned with whether it is possible to describe a universal mathematical class or set. This is something that Frege wanted to do. Each mathematical class is either a member of itself or not, although the vast majority are not. For example, the class of horses, while concerned

Rather than approach the relation of language and the world in terms of direct naming, Russell, in his influential 1905 article 'On Denoting', sets out what has since been called the 'theory of descriptions'. Russell maintained that the meaning of a sentence could be assessed solely in terms of such descriptions[8] and that those words that are usually thought of as nouns, names, or proper names do not directly pick out or latch on to things in the world; instead, they operate as a description of the properties of that thing. The word 'table' describes a piece of furniture that can be used to place items on; likewise, 'Barack Obama' is a description of the 44th President of the USA; 'King Arthur' describes a legendary figure who had a court at Camelot, a round table, etc. Such descriptions do not make sense on their own; they need to be established as part of a sentence, in the context of which they can be assessed as valid or invalid or, following Frege, as true or false.

As with Frege, Russell focuses on the role of predicates within such analyses. Predicates do not pick out or name items in the world directly; instead they designate properties or relations. It is properties, and the relations of these properties to each other, that come to the fore. Russell relied on the development of a new system of logico-mathematical notation, which he helped to develop along with Whitehead, and which enabled language to be 'translated' into a logical form. Two key examples are the existential quantifier ($\exists$), which stands for 'there exists' or 'for some object', and the universal quantifier ($\forall$), which stands

---

with horses, is not itself a horse. However, the class of classes *is* a class; that is, if you add up all the classes (that of dogs, that of cats etc.) then they will make up the class of classes. Russell pointed out to Frege the paradoxical status of a mathematical class or set which appears both to be a member of itself and not a member of itself. The problem arises with the 'class of all classes which are not members of themselves'. The question is: 'Is the class of all classes that are not members of themselves a member of itself?' If yes, no. If no, yes. Frege never adequately overcame this problem.

8. Frege had made a distinction between the 'reference' of a sentence and the 'sense' of a sentence (see Daly 2013: 38–41; Lycan 2000: 151 for a fuller discussion).

for 'for all' or 'for every'. By formalising and generalising these terms, and others, Russell (and the early Whitehead) made the first fundamental moves in enabling computer programmes to be written.[9]

For example, Russell would 'translate' a sentence such as 'The current pope is Argentinian' into the following: $\exists x[(Px \;\&\; \forall y(Py \to x = y)) \;\&\; Ax]$, where P stands for 'current pope' and A stands for the predicate 'is Argentinian'. This 'formula' then reads 'There exists something (x) which has the property of being the current pope (Px). This thing is unique ($x = y$) and all such unique things also have the property of being Argentinian (Ax).' This 'predicate' analysis, therefore, rests upon the idea that 'being the current pope' is a property that can be asserted, and assessed. The same applies to 'being Argentinian'. If these two properties are assigned to the same individual, then the sentence can be established as both meaningful and true. The current pope is Argentinian. However, such a sentence does not 'name' the pope; it describes this individual through certain properties. The key move in Russell's notion of 'definite descriptions' is the dislodging of nouns from their putative role as names for things of the world: 'their semantic values are not given by the objects (if any) which they stand for' (Miller 2007: 66). Even proper names do not operate by 'naming' but by describing a set of properties.

While some of the problematic consequences of relying on properties to account for the description or designation of the things of the world will be taken up in the following chapter, the important move that is made by both Frege and Russell is to maintain that it is sentences, or propositions, which become the objects of analysis, rather than the objects of the world. 'Russell thought in terms of sentences taken in the abstract as objects in themselves, and their logical properties in particular' (Lycan

---

9. A very well-informed and enjoyable account of the relation of the mathematical logic of Frege, Russell and Whitehead to the development of computer language is to be found in the graphic novel *Logicomix. An Epic Search for Truth* by Apostolos Doxiadis and Christos H. Papadimitriou.

2000: 22). Again, this leaves the nagging question regarding the ontological status of those objects that comprise the things of the world and that are supposedly described by propositions. Russell's focus is on the structure and strictures of language rather than attempts to describe the nature of the world, or of being. However, Russell would not be overly concerned with such questions or criticisms. Questions about the nature of the world, or of being, were, for him, reminiscent of 'metaphysics', a branch of philosophy that had fallen out of favour at the time. One reason for this was that, as Russell puts it, 'practically all metaphysics is filled with mistakes due to bad grammar' (cited in Daly 2013: 116). A rigorous, logical analysis of language would, it was supposed, do away with the mysterious problems of metaphysics. The rejection of metaphysics and the consolidation of language as the central arena and tool for philosophical and scientific analysis will be taken up in the next section.

Wittgenstein and the Vienna Circle

Another strand of the importance of the influence of both Frege and Russell is to be found in the early work of one of the greatest philosophers of the twentieth century, Ludwig Wittgenstein. Wittgenstein takes Frege's and Russell's theories on the workings of logic, language and the world to the extreme. I will cite the *whole* of chapter 1 of his monumental *Tractatus Logico-Philosophicus* (1921):

> 1 The world is all that is the case.
> 1.1 The world is the totality of facts, not of things.
> 1.11 The world is determined by the facts, and by their being *all* the facts.
> 1.12 For the totality of facts determines what is the case, and also whatever is not the case.
> 1.13 The facts in logical space are the world.
> 1.2 The world divides into facts.
> 1.21 Each item can be the case or not the case while everything else remains the same. (Wittgenstein 1974: 5)

Wittgenstein takes the logical-mathematical approach, as announced by Frege and Russell, with its emphasis on truth and falsehood, on what is or is not the case, and applies it to the whole world. This implies that the world itself is a place of logic, one made up of 'logical spaces'. The world is not made up of things but of facts. The question of truth and falsehood is not only tied to the meaning of language but is a manifestation of the world itself.[10] Wittgenstein's *Tractatus* is a marker of the philosophical attempts of the twentieth century to place logical analysis at the heart of the world.

Wittgenstein's ideas were a major influence on a group of scientists, philosophers and mathematicians originally based in Vienna in the 1920s and 1930s, and known as the Vienna Circle, whose members included Rudolf Carnap, Otto Neurath, Karl Popper and Kurt Gödel. They took the strict logical approach of Frege, Russell and Wittgenstein and extended it, aiming to rid philosophy and science of the messy, sometimes contradictory, ways in which everyday language is used. They inherited from Frege, Russell and Wittgenstein the belief that the main task was to provide an account of language in which the accuracy of its statements could be ascertained. Their overriding concern was the status of science, which was seen as the only guarantor of genuine knowledge, and they had a very specific sense of what constituted such science. The goal was to develop a 'unified science'; to cut through the superficial differences and meaningless statements of various branches of thought and to ground these in their most fundamental terms which, in this view, were to be based on logical terms. With regard to making accurate statements in science, this would involve producing a system of language in which each statement and concept could be

---

10. Later in his life, Wittgenstein rejected the central position that he had given to logical formations and developed a philosophy of language where the meaning of a word was to be seen as coming from its use, although this is somewhat of an oversimplification of the position that he developed both in his earlier work (the *Tractatus*) and his major, later book *Philosophical Investigations*.

ultimately verified by recourse to some fact. In practical terms, such facts were ultimately to be based on an observable entity; hence this approach was termed 'logical empiricism'. Again, the main enemy was the ambiguity that seems to haunt everyday language. As Wittgenstein put it in his later work: 'Philosophy is a battle against the bewitchment of our intelligence by means of our language' (Wittgenstein 1988: 109). The Vienna Circle dismissed not only metaphysics but also aesthetics and ethics.[11] Everyday language, statements about emotions, beauty, ethics and so on, were to be distrusted. Metaphysical discussions that went beyond observation were viewed as especially suspect, and were to be dismissed. Indeed, it was argued that there were no such things as genuine metaphysical problems. The task of philosophy was to clean up language, and hence clarify thought. This is a position that is set out boldly by Rudolf Carnap in an essay written in 1932 – 'The Elimination of Metaphysics Through Logical Analysis of Language'.

Later chapters will outline the need for a return not to metaphysics per se, but to an approach to language and the world that is not premised on questions of science, truth and falsehood, but is nevertheless rigorous and applicable. Ambiguity in language and in the world are not to be erased but need to be recognised and allowed for, enabled even. As Whitehead puts it, philosophy, if it is to be truly philosophical, needs to be able to account not only for matters of truth and falsehood, but also error, hesitation, imagination: 'Unfortunately theories, under their name of "propositions," have been handed over to logicians, who have countenanced the doctrine that their one function is to be judged as to their truth or falsehood [. . .] Error is the price we pay for progress' (Whitehead 1978: 184, 187). The foundations and implications of such statements will be explored in more detail in Chapters 6 and 7.

---

11. Although he was not strictly a member of the group, A. J. Ayer's 1971 book *Language, Truth and Logic* gives a vivid and entertaining account, especially in relation to ethics.

The present chapter has traced only one path from Frege to Wittgenstein, via Russell, and the analyses presented so far do not constitute a complete assessment of any of these thinkers. What is important is the reading of their work in terms of how they viewed the relation of language to the world and the role of logic within this. These thinkers signal a shift from the common-sense position in which individual words, especially nouns, are viewed as being able to pick out individual items in the world. Later in this chapter, I will try to outline some assumptions that permeate their work, and why these are problematic. Before this, I will turn to a different but consequential way of thinking about language and meaning that also developed in the early twentieth century. This involves thinking about language as a system of signs.

Language and Signs

Around the same time that Russell and Whitehead were writing *Principia Mathematica* and trying to set out the logical basis of mathematics and language, Ferdinand de Saussure was giving a series of lectures on linguistics at the University of Geneva. Although he never published a book of his own, Saussure's students collected his thoughts in their lecture notes to publish his *Course in General Linguistics* in 1916. Saussure believed that language is a system of signs, which led him to set up a new field of inquiry – semiology – which had a considerable impact on a wide range of disciplines in the twentieth century, not only in linguistics but also in social theory, philosophy, anthropology, cultural studies, psychology, sociology and anthropology.

Saussure was interested in linguistics rather than philosophy. However, he shared, with Frege and others, the desire to account for how language manages to make sense, to gain its meaning, and Saussure aimed to develop a 'scientific' (in the sense of a complete, rigorous and systematic) scheme of analysis which could be applied to various languages taken as a whole. Where

Saussure differed from Frege and his followers was that he did not see truth and falsehood or mathematical logic as key to the meaning of our words. Saussure started by investigating the way in which language works, which, he maintained, was through signification. This is a very specific version of signalling, one that does not signal things out there in the world; it is not a matter of words directly naming things. Instead, for Saussure, that which is signalled in language is the shared concepts of those people who speak that language.

According to Saussure, language is made up of signs which themselves comprise two parts: the 'signifier' and the 'signified'. The signifier is the spoken or written element: for example, the three letters 'c', 'a' and 't' put together render the signifier 'cat', which can be read or heard. The crucial point is that such a signifier does not immediately map on to a thing in the world. 'A linguistic sign is not a link between a thing and a name, but between a concept and a sound pattern' (Saussure 1983: 66). A signifier is not a name; rather it *signifies* what Saussure terms the 'signified'. Signifieds are not things or objects. In the example given above, the signified of the three letters which make up the spoken or read signifier 'cat' is the concept of 'cat'. This might involve elements (or properties, perhaps) such as 'can be kept as a pet', 'has four legs', 'is furry', 'drinks milk', 'purrs', etc. It is the amalgamation of these which the signifier signifies rather than some specific domesticated animal. Saussure calls the animal itself the 'referent'. For Saussure, the ontological status of these referents is not important for developing an understanding of how language works, for how meaning is generated. For Saussure, signifiers are conventions, a shared agreement between the speakers of a language. Different signifiers could still produce the same meaning.

Take the following sentence: 'The cat sat on the mat.' Saussure says that the signifier 'cat' makes sense to speakers of English even though there is no integral link between it and the concept of cat (the signified) or any 'real' individual, furry, milk-drinking pet (the referent). This can be seen by that fact that speakers of other languages use different words (for example, *chat* in French or *kočka* in Czech) to 'mean' the same as English speakers when they utter 'cat'. The signifier 'cat', in English, must get its sense in another way. Saussure argues that its meaning comes from the difference between this signifier and other signifiers. The signifier 'cat' gains its sense from its difference from other signifiers such as 'bat', 'hat', 'fat', 'mat' and so on. It does not take too much effort to imagine that all speakers of English could agree that the signifiers 'cat' and 'mat' signified different concepts (signifieds) to the ones that they do now. If this were the case, then the sentence 'The cat sat on the mat' could be spoken or written as 'The mat sat on the cat', but we would still have the same meaning; that of an animal resting on some cloth, not some cloth resting on an animal.

Saussure takes this argument further, stating that it is not only signifiers that are arbitrary. Signifieds (concepts) are as well, to an extent. Although it may appear that each language has a different set of signs that somehow signify the same 'thing' (cat, *chat*, *kočka*), this is not Saussure's view: 'if words had the job of representing concepts fixed in advance, one would be able to find exact equivalents for them as between one language and another. But this is not the case' (Saussure 1983: 114–15). Different words in different languages have different shades or values, even if they have the same meaning.[12] For example, the word *Schadenfreude* has been imported into English from German to convey the feeling of pleasure that we take in the misfortune of others. What Saussure says about the arbitrary character of signifiers also applies to signifieds, to concepts. They, too, are a matter of convention rather than logical expressions of the way

---

12. 'The French word *mouton* may have the same meaning as the English word *sheep*; but it does not have the same value. There are various reasons for this, but in particular the fact that the English word for the meat of this animal, as prepared and served for a meal, is not *sheep* but *mutton*. The difference in value between *sheep* and *mouton* hinges on the fact that in English there is also another word *mutton* for the meat, whereas *mouton* in French covers both' (Saussure 1983: 114).

the world is (as Frege and his followers would have it). It is for this reason, perhaps, that the work of Saussure was taken up so avidly in social and cultural theory throughout the twentieth century. His ideas stress the role of groups or communities in deciding upon, or being influenced by, the categories that make up how we see and speak of the world. Language is a system of signs that it is possible to scrutinise and analyse. For example, Roland Barthes (1915–80) extended Saussure's semiological approach and applied it to advertisements, wrestling and striptease, among other phenomena, and related the signs of contemporary society to the operations and continuation of capitalism. The French anthropologist Claude Lévi-Strauss (1908–2009) also made use of Saussure's theory of signs and applied it to the analysis of different cultures around the world (see, for example, Lévi-Strauss 1994).

That language, as a system of signs, is not concerned with the truth or falsehood of the statements that speakers of that language make might seem to imply that language is not based on logical forms, as was the case for Frege and Russell. This does not, however, entail that language and its meanings cannot be analysed logically. In setting up the field of semiotics, Saussure was trying to provide a rigorous analysis of language into its component signs. To this end, he invented a range of important technical terms such as 'synchronic' and 'diachronic', '*langue*' and '*parole*', 'syntagms' and 'paradigms'. However, he was firm in his stance that just because signs can be analysed logically does not mean that they, and the world, are inherently logical (as Wittgenstein suggested). Instead, and as mentioned above, Saussure argued that language was, in a very distinct sense, 'arbitrary'.

To return to the biblical story of Adam naming the animals, it was left undecided as to whether these names somehow picked out the true essence of each animal or whether they were simply invented by Adam and, hence, could have been different. It is this contingency that identifies the arbitrary character of language. The work of Frege, Russell and Saussure has moved away from the idea that language is intimately linked to the character of the individual items to which it refers, or appears to name. For

30

Frege, sentences are quasi-abstract and the meaning of sentences comes not from the accuracy of reference to things in the world but from their status within the realm of the 'True and the False'. Like Frege, Saussure maintains that concepts (signifieds) are the key to understanding the way language works, but he does not require the logico-mathematical approach to establish his systematic (scientific) analysis; like Russell, he appears to be interested in properties, but unlike Russell, his concern is the properties of concepts rather than objects.

Conclusion

This chapter has outlined two contrasting approaches to language whose legacies have been far-reaching in twentieth- and early twenty-first-century thought. In their different ways, both sought to go beyond the belief that words directly grasp, capture, refer to, denote or name the things of the world. The logical-mathematical approach of Frege and his descendants maintains that language, and its meaningfulness, should be seen as a matter of establishing the truth or falsehood of language statements or propositions. For Saussure and his followers in the fields of social and cultural analysis, language and meaning are made up of a system of signs. These signs permeate all elements of culture, films, adverts, fashion and so on, and can be 'read' using the tools of semiotics developed by Saussure. Although the logical and semiotic approaches to language are very different, they have one thing in common: it is impossible to talk directly of the things of the world. According to Frege, to state that 'the planet Earth has one moon' is to assign the value 'one' to the predicate 'moon of Earth'.[13] This can then be judged to be true or false. For Russell,

---

13. Weiner (2004: 56) explains Frege's specific approach to the status and function of language through the example of the sentence 'Venus has 0 (zero) moons.' What is being asserted in such an instance? Frege's response is to state that such a statement is not directly about Venus. Rather than

to state that 'the planet Earth has one moon' is a set of definite descriptions that attain a logical consistency that, again, can be judged as true or false. For Saussure, it is concepts, not things or objects, that are signified by the signifiers that we write or speak. To state that 'the planet Earth has one moon' is not to directly indicate an object in the night sky, but to signal a shared concept of what a specific culture understands by the sign 'moon'. The content of this concept can change, as society changes; it used to be made of cheese, it is now a place that humans have visited. In Frege, Russell and Saussure's accounts, the things of the world are not directly accessible through language.

The logical-mathematical approach says that language gets its meaning from sentences, not individual words. The semiological approach calls the things of the world 'referents' and declares that they play no real role in language, which is really a matter of signifiers and signifieds. An extreme version of the latter position can be found in the work of the psychoanalyst and theorist Jacques Lacan (1901–81) who applied Saussure's ideas to Freud's notion of the unconscious. Lacan believed that words (signs) are absolutely primary over things, for example, when he states: 'It is the world of words that creates the world of things' (Lacan 1977: 65).

To my mind, the inability of words to talk of the things of the world is a problem, one that will be taken up throughout this book, where I will argue that one reason why both of these approaches gave up on the things of the world and turned to questions of truth or signification is that they have made some

---

directly stating that 'Venus has 0 moons' (Venus has no moons), a numerical value is given to a concept. In this case the concept is 'moon of Venus' and the value of zero has been ascribed to it. This concept could have been given the value of one or two or three, but on this occasion it has been given the value of 0 (zero). Frege provides another example: 'If I say "the King's carriage is drawn by four horses", then I assign the number four to the concept "horse that drives the King's carriage"' (cited in Harrison 1979: 53). Crucially, Frege maintains that this applies not only to numbers but to all sentences.

rather telling assumptions about what it is to be a thing. Things are taken to be static objects that exist in their own right and in their own way. Language operates either as a logical system that is divorced from such things (Frege), as a self-consistent description of the properties of such things (Russell), or as a general agreement within a certain group upon the relation between specific signifiers and signifieds rather than between signs and things (Saussure). In all such theories, a gap has been created between the world and human language. The joint solution was to let the things of the world and the world of things become a secondary consideration, to slip into the background, although in diverse ways and for different reasons. All these approaches tacitly bear witness to the problem of correlationism, where thought or language always mediate access to things-in-themselves.

Is it not possible to think of things and of the world differently, and so to think about the place of language in the world in a more productive manner, one that avoids bifurcations and the temptations of correlationism? Answering this question will take up the rest of this book.

3

Adjectives: The Properties of the World and the 'Bifurcation of Nature'

The previous chapter identified certain problems associated with explaining the relation between language and the things of the world in terms of names or signification. This chapter will look at a related question (as partially raised by Russell), namely, is it possible to talk accurately of the properties or qualities of the things of the world? A world of nouns alone would be a lifeless place with no characteristics or qualities. There would be no colours, no warmth, no size. Yet we are immersed in a world with a vast array of different properties. A specific class of words, namely adjectives, is deployed to describe how 'terrible', 'beautiful', 'green', 'tiny', 'enormous' or even 'mundane' things are. This chapter will outline a range of ideas and theories which have attempted to explain the relationship of human perception to the properties of things (or objects). In doing so, it will also introduce Whitehead's notion of the 'bifurcation of nature' which, although similar to aspects of Meillassoux's diagnosis of the correlationist circle, offers a distinct and more productive way of approaching this problem.

The Thingness of Things

It may have been noted that in the earlier pages, the word 'thing' has been used extensively, as well as the phrase 'things of the world', without any definition being provided. One reason for this is that the word 'thing' is open and not wedded to any specific standpoint or theory. All of the following could be said to be things, in one way or another: democracy, bottles, beetles, buttons, marriage, complex financial instruments such as futures, hope, despair, lust. Whitehead made a similar point when he stated that 'I am using the word "thing" in its most general sense, which can include activities, colours [. . .] and values. In this sense, "thing" is whatever we can talk about' (Whitehead 1938: 193). There is a second reason for the use of thing, in preference to the word 'object'.[1] As Latour (1993) made clear, there is a striking difference between the words 'thing' and 'object'.[2] While things have been around for a long time, objects are of more recent origin.

The current meaning of the word 'object' might be defined as 'a tangible and visible thing' (as given in the *Collins English Dictionary*). This meaning of the word only came to the fore between the fifteenth and sixteenth centuries, at the birth of the Scientific Revolution and the very start of the Enlightenment. A key aspect of such a definition is that objects must be presented to the senses, must be able to be seen or touched. This is linked to a specific rendering of what constitutes knowledge, one based on empiricism. Moreover, an object is known through the perception of its *properties* through their presentation to, or via, the senses. The prioritisation of knowledge in relation to objects grants them a different epistemological and ontological status to things. Objects are *objects of knowledge* and, consequently, of study.

---

1. Martin Heidegger (1869–1976) directly addresses this relation in a chapter called 'The Thing' in his book *Poetry, Language, Thought*. However, his approach differs from mine in that I see the difference as a historical, conceptual one, rather than a difference between what a thing is for itself and in its relation to humans.
2. Bruno Latour has made things a special study of his work. He argues that the social sciences, cultural studies and even science itself have not paid enough attention to things. We have tended to think that they are mute and passive and do not have the capacity to act. As will be seen in the next section, there has been a tendency to reduce things to objects. See, for example, Latour's contentious but enticing 1993 book *We Have Never Been Modern*.

For example, hope, courage, republics, democracy, unicorns, fairies, séances and religion can all be referred to as things, in one sense or another. It is not immediately clear that they are objects, as they cannot all be touched, seen, defined, isolated, 'known'. Yet it is possible to render such things as objects, by placing them within a field of knowledge, or study. Hence, a psychologist might study hope and courage as objects that are somehow contained in the minds of individuals or groups. Political scientists might study republics and democracies. Literary scholars might study the use of unicorns and fairies in the work of Shakespeare. Sociologists might study the role of séances or religion in different cultures and societies. These things have been translated into objects by being placed in a specialised arena, to which only trained experts have access.

The objects that science studies are defined as having specific properties. They can be seen, touched, measured, weighed, tested. They are fixed rather than capricious. Iron might change under different conditions, at different temperatures, for example, but it does so in a way that can be measured and predicted; it does not change on its own whim. Iron has a certain set of properties that make it what it is. Knowledge of these properties is knowledge of iron considered as an object (not simply as a thing).[3] The democratic aspect of things, which seemed to be open to everyone, has been lost. Things have been made into objects of knowledge, and only a few have the ability to talk accurately of them, to know them.

On this view, objects are objects precisely insofar as they have a specific set of properties that can be known. In this sense, objects are 'self-identical'; they are what they are, and they are where they are. No other information is needed to understand them. However, as will be seen in the next section, this seemingly

---

3. As will be seen in later chapters, Whitehead would disagree with such a position. For him, 'There is no such thing as iron at an instant; to be iron is a character of an event' (Whitehead 1919: 23). The implications of such statements will be taken up in Chapters 4 and 5.

simple position, in which objects are defined by their properties, is not so easy to justify. Moreover, some of the problems associated with such an approach are linked to the way that language is organised, especially with regard to adjectives.

The Problem of 'Primary Substance'

To state that 'this water has a temperature of 100 °C' is to assign a specific property (temperature) to a specific entity (water). The water is the 'subject' of the sentence, and temperature is 'predicated' of it (see the analysis of Frege and Russell in Chapter 2). Whitehead refers to this as the 'subject–predicate' axis. Those languages, such as English, that are structured in such a way to grant priority to subject–predicate formulations might appear to reflect an uncontroversial approach to knowing the world, where an entity is posited and properties are assigned to such an entity. 'For example consider the type of propositions such as "The grass is green," and "The whale is big." This subject–predicate form of statement seems so simple, leading straight to a metaphysical first principle; and yet in these examples it conceals such complex, diverse meanings' (Whitehead 1978: 13). The assumption is that there are fixed entities to which changeable properties can be ascribed. According to Whitehead, there is a danger in taking the linguistic structure of the subject–predicate axis and assuming that it represents how the world actually *is*. This runs the risk of simplifying the diversity of existence by reducing all instances to the same logical structure, that of the subject–predicate axis. It also allows correlationism to gain a foothold. Although Whitehead does not develop his critique in the same manner as Meillassoux, he would agree that this conception of the relation between language and being is problematic: 'the exclusive reliance on sense-perception promotes a false metaphysics' (Whitehead 1933: 281), as it assumes that beneath experience there is a fundamental ground that quietly subtends that experience. This establishes an erroneous, or problematic, viewpoint where it is the attributes of matter rather than matter itself that is presented to humans and from which knowledge is derived.

Unlike Meillassoux, who lays the blame for all aspects of correlationism at the door of Kant, Whitehead traces this specific conflation of the organisation of language, grammar and existence to the metaphysics and logic of Aristotle.[4] On Whitehead's reading, Aristotle takes the simplest form of sentences as indicating how the world really is (Whitehead 1933: 169). Aristotle assumes that all existence is made up of something fixed and inert that has certain properties ('it is hot', 'it is cold'). He separates this 'it' from its properties. Whitehead describes this 'it' as alluding to what Aristotle termed 'primary substance'. The properties of an object, and the words (most often adjectives) used to describe these, might change, but somehow 'it', the object, remains the same. 'The unquestioned acceptance of the Aristotelian logic has led to an ingrained tendency to postulate a sub-stratum for whatever is disclosed in sense awareness, namely, to look below what we are aware of for the substance in the sense of the "concrete thing"' (Whitehead 1964: 18). The subject–predicate axis posits a ground that comprises utter reality and that exists separately from the perceptions, thoughts and conceptions of (human) subjects; it is modelled on the positing of a primary substance that subtends the qualities or characteristics that are attributed to it. This is manifest in the adjectives that are used to designate the properties, qualities or attributes that are predicated of a primary substance.

Whitehead states that the influence of Aristotle is not only widespread but pernicious. 'The evil produced by Aristotelian "primary substance" is exactly this habit of metaphysical emphasis upon the "subject–predicate" form of propositions' (Whitehead 1978: 30). Once more, a gulf has been created between the world-as-it-is and information about the world-as-it-is, leading

---

4. Though, as will be seen in later chapters, Whitehead traces different aspects and routes of a range of bifurcations.

to the latent but pervasive correlationist difficulty where there is a resolute disjunction between what a thing is for itself and its presentation (for knowledge) to human subjects, as outlined by Meillassoux (2008). Or, as Whitehead puts it: 'All modern epistemologies, all modern cosmologies, wrestle with this problem. There is, for their doctrine, a mysterious reality in the background, intrinsically unknowable by any direct intercourse' (Whitehead 1933: 170).

This epistemological problem also haunts contemporary science. The subject–predicate axis may have been a workable hypothesis for the kind of Newtonian science that was undertaken from roughly the seventeenth to the end of the nineteenth centuries; for example, it works well when thinking about how the planets orbit the sun. However, Whitehead maintains that to think of the universe as only made up of such objects (planets, suns, moons) is a very specific, even limited, way of thinking. It might work on some occasions but it is not a complete account. Contemporary science does not always study such objects; it now investigates energy, vibrations, waves. The concept of objects is inadequate to describe a universe 'created' by a big bang, a universe that is replete with flows of energy. Moreover, some of the particles that contemporary physics has identified, such as photons, do not have any mass. Yet Whitehead believes that scientists still often think in the old Aristotelian way, and that this hampers them. Scientists have not completely rid their language and thoughts of the idea that the world is fundamentally made up of objects. Whitehead puts this point boldly when he writes: 'in the present-day reconstruction of physics fragments of the Newtonian concepts are stubbornly retained. The result is to reduce modern physics to a sort of mystic chant over an unintelligible Universe' (Whitehead 1938: 152). This is perhaps why there are such problems when thinking about the status of photons. Sometimes they appear to be particles (objects), sometimes they appear to be waveforms (not objects but vectors of energy). 'The story commences with the wave-theory of light and ends with the wave-theory of matter' (Whitehead 1933: 200).

In order to avoid such problems, it is first necessary to trace another path through which the disjunction between matter and its properties was established. This is through the mixing of philosophical and scientific ideas in the late seventeenth century, in the work of John Locke (1632–1704) and the natural philosopher (or physicist in today's parlance) Isaac Newton (1642–1727).

The Problem of Primary and Secondary Qualities

To state that things have certain properties and that adjectives seem the best way to describe such properties might seem a straightforward, almost common-sense, position – when it actually reflects a specific metaphysical stance, one that is committed to a specific way of speaking, thinking and acting. It is a position that is, perhaps, mostly clearly set out by John Locke in his influential book *An Essay Concerning Human Understanding*, written in 1690, three years after Isaac Newton had published his own major work, *Mathematical Principles of Natural Knowledge*. Newton's book introduced a range of ideas about force, mass, acceleration, as well as his three laws of motion and his theory of gravity. During the period between the sixteenth and seventeenth centuries, the era of the Scientific Revolution, there was no clear split between what counted as a philosophical question and what was a purely scientific one. Locke was an acquaintance of Newton and they were interested in the same kind of problems. Newton had proposed that light and sound were *transmitted* from one object to another. Although Newton was not aware of the waveform of light and sound,[5] his theory that light and sound were transmitted was radical and far-reaching.[6]

5. Newton believed that light was transmitted in the form of 'corpuscles' which left the object and entered the eye.
6. In his earlier work, Newton had established a link between light and colour by using a prism to 'split' white light into its component parts. Strictly speaking, his innovation was to use a second prism to refract the light that had been split by a first prism. He used a lens and a second prism to

Indeed, it was into the new mix of experiments, theories and findings in the seventeenth century about how light and sound were transmitted from one object to another (and, most importantly, from objects to humans) that Locke offered his account of primary and secondary qualities.

Locke argues that objects have two different kinds of properties. Some properties are integral to that object; other properties appear to be more contingent, as they rely upon human perception (sight, taste, smell, etc.). Locke calls the first set 'primary qualities' and those that are not integral to the object 'secondary qualities'. Examples of primary qualities are shape and size. Secondary qualities involve colour, taste and smell. This entails that objects have some properties that always belong to them, whether we see them, touch them, hear them, smell them, taste them or not. These primary qualities comprise what that object really *is* and provide a grounding for secondary qualities. As such, secondary qualities 'are nothing in the objects themselves, but the power to produce various sensations in us by their *primary qualities*' (Locke 1997: 135, emphasis in original).

Locke's rather deft account seemed to explain how objects could have their own properties that remain the same, and yet also transmit a different set of properties such as colour and light to humans. Both sets of properties are real, but they are *of a different kind*. Locke's apparent solution to this problem contributed to philosophical and scientific outlooks over the next few hundred years. It was also linked, integrally, to language. Nouns designate objects in terms of their integral existence (primary qualities), while adjectives describe the changeable, inessential, properties (secondary qualities) of such objects.

What I have said concerning *colours* and *smells*, may be understood also of *tastes*, and *sounds*, *and other sensible qualities*; which,

---

recompose the 'split' colours of light back into one 'white' ray. In this way he showed that the colour was a property of light itself (not something given to the light by the prism).

whatever reality we by mistake, attribute to them, are in truth nothing in the objects themselves, but powers to produce various sensations in us, and *depend on those primary qualities.* (Locke 1997: 136, emphases in original)

This leads to the question of which properties always belong to an object and which are more superficial or changeable. If an object is known via its presentation to the senses, then it should be possible to list the properties that are thus presented. However, a problem arises when attempting to distinguish between those properties that inhere in the object and those that appear to be changeable. A good example is that of colours (which themselves are closely related to adjectives).

A piece of cloth may appear red when observed at midday. However, in the dusk it may appear to be orange; at night it could appear black. If it is put a sealed chest, how is it possible to know what colour it is? It seems that the colour of a thing is variable which, in turn, suggests that colour is not a fixed property of the cloth. The appearance of colour seems to be reliant upon its perception (by a human), and the conditions in which such perception occurs. If this is the case, then if no one sees the cloth, can it be said to have any colour at all? If there are contingent properties that rely more on the perceiver than the perceived, then if the perceiver is not present, such properties may well not be present either.

Properties such as colours appear to be reliant upon human perception, thought and language. This leaves a gap between such human-based perception and the object itself. Secondary qualities may be perceived, known, talked of, but the primary qualities that 'generate' them and that constitute the thing-in-itself remain unknown, hidden, inaccessible. This raises the question of what colour the object is (or has) *for itself?* What is it in the object that is actually red? Is red a thing or the property of a thing? Locke's theory suggests that the object has the capacity to be viewed as red, under the appropriate conditions, but until it is perceived as red, it is not strictly correct to say that it *is* red.

Secondary qualities involve not only properties based on sight, such as colours, but also other properties such as sound and taste. Salt has a specific taste that can be described with the adjective 'salty'. Does this mean that salt is *salty*, even when no one is eating it? Does it taste salty in the same way to goats and horses as it does to humans? The discovery of atoms and molecules since the time when Locke was writing has not overcome such questions, but has made them more intractable. Table salt is (mostly) made up of sodium chloride, which itself is a molecule comprising ionised sodium and chlorine atoms. Many would say that this specific molecular structure is an essential property (a primary quality) of sodium chloride (and hence table salt). Is the salty taste of salt, likewise, an integral property of sodium chloride, in the same way that its molecular structure is? Is the saltiness really *there*, in each individual salt molecule? Or is it some kind of human-based secondary quality?

With regard to sound, examples of a contemporary rendering of secondary qualities can be found in some psychological approaches to the status of music. For example, the neuroscientist Daniel Levitin is adamant that music, musical structures, pitch, scales of tones, etc. do not exist 'in nature'; they are products of a brain that interprets physical (primary) qualities in specific ways. 'Sound waves – molecules of air vibrating at various frequencies – do not themselves have pitch [. . .] it takes a human (or animal) brain to map them [. . .] We perceive colour in a similar way [. . .] Newton was the first to point out that light is colourless' (Levitin 2006: 22). Although Levitin seems to allow for the wider possibility of animals also interpreting primary qualities in such a way, his main argument is to do with the relation of the human brain to the frequencies of the world. His approach is quite severe, in that music becomes so secondary that it appears almost illusory: 'Music, then, can be thought of as a type of perceptual illusion in which our brain imposes structure and order on a sequence of sounds' (Levitin 2006: 109). Levitin's position extends the reach of the notion of secondary qualities. It signals a split between a purported factuality of nature and the human brain, mind, or subject which then interprets the supposedly factual world in various ways. As will be seen in the next section, this is a firm example of what Whitehead calls the bifurcation of nature.[7]

Whitehead and the 'Bifurcation of Nature'

Locke's specific rendering of perception of the world in terms of primary and secondary qualities has contributed to the construction of a specific concept of reality, in which objects carry their own integral properties that are distinct from those properties via which humans perceive them, although some kind of dependence of the latter is presumed, even if not well-defined (Debaise 2017: 12). This is reflected in the view that modern science studies what the world is really like, involving analyses of the facts and objects of the world. This approach is envisaged

---

7. It is worth outlining an early response to the problem of secondary qualities, as set out by Bishop George Berkeley (1685–1783). Occasionally, in films or television programmes, the following, supposedly philosophical, question is raised: 'If a tree falls in a wood and there is no one there to hear it, does it make a noise?' This is often put in a facetious manner. However, Levitin's (and many other psychologists') approach to music, where music is seen as some kind of 'perceptual illusion', demonstrates that this question still has bite. The surface level of this question suggests that if there is really a distinction between primary and secondary qualities, and if secondary qualities involve *all* instances of light, sound, touch etc., then the things of the world (objects) must in themselves have no colour and make no noise. There is also a deeper level to this question. If it is accepted that secondary qualities are solely reliant upon human perception, if it is agreed that they describe how humans are acquainted with the world, then how can a distinction ever be made between such secondary qualities and primary qualities? To put it another way: what is it that tells us what is primary and what is secondary about a quality? If the information that is received about the world comes from sight, touch, hearing, etc., that is, from secondary qualities, then surely the information that we gather about supposed primary qualities also comes in this 'secondary' way. This would suggest that all qualities are secondary ones and to state that there are primary ones below these is to go beyond the evidence.

as different in kind to those analyses of the world that focus on its appearance to humans, as investigated by the fields of literary studies, aesthetics, anthropology, cultural studies, and certain approaches to sociology.

Whitehead describes this splitting of the world into two different camps as the 'bifurcation of nature' (Whitehead 1964: 26–48). It is worth noting that the very specific concept of the bifurcation of nature is one that Whitehead introduces in his book *The Concept of Nature* (1920) as a way of addressing certain problems within the philosophy of science. When Whitehead moves beyond this to a wider, metaphysical analysis in *Process and Reality* (1929), he states that his position now not only 'embodies a protest against the "bifurcation" of nature. It embodies even more than that: its protest is against the bifurcation of actualities' (Whitehead 1978: 289). Clearly, Whitehead is not disavowing his earlier concept (the bifurcation of nature), but extending its reach. As will be seen in later chapters, there are various aspects and renditions of such bifurcations (mind/body, language/world, 'sex'/gender) which need to be accounted for on their own terms, and not reduced to a catch-all concept. As Debaise (2017: 11–13) has made clear, bifurcation is not limited to one event or theory; it is an *operation* in both thought and action that permeates and manifests itself in a wide range of ideas, outlooks and approaches.

Locke's discussion of primary and secondary qualities is one of the clearest examples of what is involved in such operations. It is for this reason that Whitehead comments of Locke's theory that 'It seems an extremely unfortunate arrangement that we should perceive a lot of things that are not there. Yet this is what the theory of secondary qualities in fact comes to' (Whitehead 1964: 27). Whitehead's outline and critique of the bifurcation of nature does not view it as a one-off event, nor it is a 'fact' that can be identified. It is expressed in a manner of thought,[8] one

---

8. The importance of analysing the manner, or mode, of thinking has been discussed extensively by Debaise (2017) and will be taken up in Chapter 5.

that is both inconsistent and untenable, as it comprises a 'radical inconsistency at the basis of thought [that] accounts for much that is half-hearted and wavering in our civilisation. It would be going too far to say that it distracts thought. It enfeebles it, by reason of the inconsistency lurking in the background' (Whitehead 1932: 94). For example, the perception of a green leaf or a piece of silver appears to involve the perception of a leaf that *is* green and a piece of silver that *is* silver in colour. However, these colours are deemed by Locke (and modern science) to be merely secondary properties of these things. The leaf itself is not green (its molecules are not green) and nor is the piece of silver. Silver is not *silver*. The further that physics ventures into the realm of the subatomic, and insists that it is uncovering the secrets of 'reality', the more peculiar the situation becomes. When the term 'theoretical physics' arose in the early twentieth century it signalled a break with the mechanical physics that had been prevalent in the nineteenth century (see Stengers 2010: 259–61). There was a shift from direct experimentation to the use of abstract, mathematical techniques to uncover the true secrets of the universe, where 'reality' really lies. Yet the further the findings of theoretical physics take us, the less 'real' they seem to be.

Theoretical physics quickly went beyond what humans can see and touch (colours, hardness, etc.) to the atomic and sub-atomic level, which could not be seen or touched but only inferred by various complex devices (electron microscopes, the Hadron Collider, etc.) and read off via technical instruments or computers. There are now phenomena that even such technical devices cannot 'see', but which have to be presupposed for current theories to work (as was the case for the long-elusive Higgs boson). Over the last thirty years or so, it has become apparent that the matter that we can see and touch only makes up a small percentage of existence (approximately 4%); the rest is made up of 'dark matter' (23%) and 'dark energy' (73%), on recent counts. Science would still claim that such phenomena also comprise a real 'reality'. Whitehead describes such an approach not as theoretical physics but, instead, as 'speculative physics' (Whitehead 1964: 30). This is not to dismiss physics or to suggest that physicists are simply making things up. It does, however, point to the need for an appreciation of the limits of physics: 'the wave-theory of light is an excellent well-established theory; but unfortunately it leaves out colour as perceived. Thus the perceived redness – or, other colour – has to be cut out of nature and made into the reaction of the mind' (Whitehead 1964: 46).

The real problem comes when physics posits that it alone has the right and authority to make declarations on what is 'really real'. By insisting that what is really real lies beyond our perceptions and in the realm of the subatomic, physics denies that human perceptions of the world, of green leaves, red sunsets and silver pieces of silver, are really real. It also denies the experiences of all other organisms, plants and animals on planet Earth or elsewhere. This reasserts a specific and powerful bifurcation, one that should not be acceptable to philosophy, for, unlike physics, philosophy cannot reduce reality to the subatomic; it needs to be able to incorporate all experience. As Whitehead puts it: 'We cannot pick and choose. For us the red glow of the sunset should be as much part of nature as are the molecules and electric waves by which men [*sic*] of science would explain this phenomenon' (Whitehead 1964: 29). Chapters 4, 5 and 6 will explore some of the ways in which it might be possible to incorporate such apparently subjective secondary qualities within both language and the 'real' world, through analyses of the work of Deleuze, Dewey, Whitehead and Irigaray.

The seeming paradox is that modern physics suggests that our usual conception of objects as self-contained and fixed is incorrect or lacking, as the universe is made up of waves of energy that coalesce at points to form the subatomic particles that, in turn, come together to make up the atoms and molecules of the world that, eventually, comprise the things that we see. The objects of the world are not, therefore, solid, but are ultimately made up of vibrations, waves, resonances. 'All that is

solid melts into air.'[9] However, the way we think and speak of
such a world remains as it ever was. It relies on the assumption that there is a fixed base, a 'primary substance' (apparently
designated by nouns) that can be described (by using adjectives
to assign different properties to it). The perception of a blue
car is rendered as a personal, private or subjective experience.
The shade of blue of the car is contingent, as it could have been
green or red or black, while the 'it' of the car itself would have
remained the same. As discussed previously, this harks back to
Aristotle's view of logic and its relationship to how our language
is organised. Through the work of writers such as Locke and
Newton, this approach had a direct influence on the development of the modern scientific attitude from the seventeenth
century onwards. This deeply ingrained way of thinking and
speaking limits our view of the world. The task is to think
otherwise: 'My present point is that sky-blue is found in nature
with a definite implication in events' (Whitehead 1964: 15).

Although the way our language is structured might seem
to suggest otherwise, things and their properties always come
together, all at once. 'You cannot know what is red by merely
thinking of redness. You can only find red things by adventur-
ing amid physical experiences in *this* actual world' (Whitehead
1978: 256). Things and their properties never were and never
are separate. There are only ever blue cars, red cars, green cars;
colourless cars just do not exist; there is no bare 'it' beneath cars.
Our sentences may want to fix the world into a set of nouns
and then use adjectives to describe these, but that is not how the
world *is*.

---

9. This is a something that Marx said regarding how capitalism sweeps away
   our old certainties about society, the economy and the nature of things.
   The relation of Marx to questions of process and language will be taken up
   in Chapter 8.

Conclusion

As may well have been noted, the last two chapters of this book have been quite critical. They have indicated a range of problems with language and its relation to the world. They have pointed to the difficulties in accounting for the seemingly simple issue of how words latch on to the world, and the problems associated with separating things from their properties, nouns from their adjectives. The following chapters will be more positive as they will suggest that it is possible to use some of the tools already inherent in language to produce more adequate and productive ways of thinking about the world. Poets and poetry have, for centuries, been trying to manipulate language, to bring about new kinds of reactions to the world.

The seventeenth-century poet Andrew Marvell (1621–78), in his poem 'The Garden', wrote of 'Annihilating all that's made / To a green thought in a green shade' (1982: 257). Marvell does not separate the properties of the world from thought: both are green. Greenness is in the thing (the garden) and in the way it is thought (a green thought).[10] This is not to imply that philosophy and science need to resort to poetry, but to ignore this resource would be to accept the bifurcation of nature at face value, and to render poetry as unable to provide accurate or important information. Nor is it to declare that properties and things are always tied together; it is to suggest the need to investigate other elements of language as ways of thinking about the world. As has been discussed in the two previous chapters, analyses of both language and the world have been dogged by the assumption that there are static objects in the world that have properties that change. I would suggest that it is worth bringing other aspects to the fore such as 'what happens?' and '*how* do things happen?'

---

10. Another, more recent poet, Wallace Stevens (1879–1955), also attempted to redescribe the activity of adjectives in language and in the world in his poem *The Man with the Blue Guitar*. This will be discussed further in Chapter 5.

The following two chapters will approach the questions of 'what happens?' and 'how does it happen?' through a discussion of verbs and adverbs.

4

Verbs: Deleuze on Infinitives, Events and Process

At one point in *Process and Reality*, Whitehead borrows an epithet from William James and declares that 'We find ourselves in a buzzing world, amid a democracy of fellow creatures; whereas under some disguise or other, orthodox philosophy can only introduce us to solitary substances, each enjoying an illusory experience' (Whitehead 1978: 50). Previous chapters have outlined some of the ways in which philosophy has prioritised such 'solitary substances' in terms of individual items of existence, things or objects, which are designated or described by nouns and whose integral characters have become divorced from their perceptions by other entities. The properties that are assigned to such objects have a problematic status; they appear to be not just secondary, but illusory, creations of the perceiver rather than the perceived. In this way, the problem of correlationism is allowed to enter the scene. Objects are unknowable in themselves and human experience always refers back to itself via either thought or language. This chapter, following Whitehead, will turn to the 'buzzing world' in which things *happen*. This notion of happening will move the discussion from the supposed primacy of self-identical objects to the eventful character of existence. It will use the concept of verbs, especially in their infinitive or infinite mode, as discussed by Gilles Deleuze (1925–95), to develop this line of thought.

The Question of Process

The idea of process has had its place in the work of many philosophers, although it is a notion that has often been neglected. The Ancient Greek philosopher Heraclitus sums up one aspect when he famously said: 'You cannot step into the same river twice.'[1] Because a river flows, by definition its waters are always changing and it is therefore impossible to step into exactly the same river again. What makes a river a river is that its waters are always different. A river is constantly in flow, in flux. Heraclitus extends this idea and says that everything that exists 'flows' or is in a state of constant change.

This view of the world as constantly in flux has never predominated in philosophy but has been present in the work of a range of writers such as Baruch de Spinoza (1632–77), Karl Marx (1818–83), Henri Bergson (1859–1941) and, most notably for this book, Alfred North Whitehead. In the latter years of the twentieth century, a renewed interest in such ideas developed and a related term, 'event',[2] was revisited. The concept of event is hard to define, to pin down, precisely because our language and thought have prioritised knowledge of static objects (through nouns), and have attempted to describe their properties (through adjectives). As a result, the very concepts of process and event, with their associated notions of movement and change, are hard to isolate or capture. It is because movement and change inhere in existence that attempts to render process or events as objects of inspection are problematic. As Whitehead once remarked in a lecture: 'Reality is becoming . . . Can't catch a moment by the scruff of the neck – it's gone' (cited in Ford 1984: 265).

Nevertheless, there is still a need, a requirement even, to develop accounts that can approach the notions of process and

---

1. At least this is how Plato reported the words of Heraclitus in his dialogue *Cratylus* (Plato 2014).
2. A very good and clear review of recent discussions of the concept of the event can be found in Fraser (2006).

event. This chapter will suggest that one such approach can be found in the activity of verbs. It will not attempt to provide prior definitions of either 'event' or 'process'. These terms will be treated as challenges, or alternatives, to the more usual conceptions of objects and subjects. The aim is to map out a way of bypassing the problems associated with viewing the world as constituted by objects that are known by (human) subjects (with the associated pitfall of correlationism). The desire or temptation to fall back into establishing prior definitions of event or process could be seen as symptomatic of the prevalence of static categories of thought that aim to capture the essence, being or character of the world through nouns and adjectives.

Infinitives and Infinity

Textbooks for students learning a (European) language will often categorise and list verbs in their infinitive form. This form does not imply that any person or thing is carrying out the action of the verb; nor does it indicate when the action is being carried out. Some examples of the infinitive form of verbs are 'to eat', 'to drive' and 'to do'. It is this lack of any reference to a specific time, person or thing that makes the verb 'infinitive', which, in turn, introduces the notion of the *infinite*.

As will be seen, Deleuze does not deny that language has specific qualities, but he does not view language as a solely human creation or affair. Language bears witness to, and is located within, the eventful character of existence. 'Events make language possible' (Deleuze 1990: 181). In *The Logic of Sense*, Deleuze develops this argument by making a distinction between two different aspects of all verbs: 'the present' and 'the infinitive' (1990: 184). 'The verb has two poles: the present, which indicates its relation to a denotable state of affairs [. . .] and the infinitive, which indicates its relation to sense of the event' (Deleuze 1990: 184). 'The present' encompasses those elements that have already been addressed in the work of writers such as

Frege and Saussure. Deleuze maintains that this only indicates one aspect of the operation of verbs. Deleuze's notion of the present will be returned to after a fuller analysis of his development of the infinitive element of verbs, which he maintains has been overlooked within philosophy, especially the philosophy of language.

Deleuze sets aside, temporarily, the individual instances of verbs in order to focus on their infinitive forms, such as 'to eat', 'to drive' or 'to do'. These forms, he argues, indicate an, as yet, untapped potential. Anything could technically do the eating, driving or doing. And they could do so at any point – in the past, the present or the future. Unlike those thinkers who start with human language and then wonder how this applies to, or refers to, the world, Deleuze sees language as intimately tied up with the world, with the events of the world: 'the infinitive verb expresses the event of language – language being a unique event which merges now with that which renders it possible' (Deleuze 1990: 185). For Deleuze, human language is not creative in any originary sense and nor is it unique. Because language is possible, because it exists, this must say something about the wider world, about existence itself, as language is part of existence. In so far as the undetermined infinite verb expresses language as an event, it should be treated as eventful in the same way that other events are eventful. Rather than treat language as separate from the world, the question to ask is what it must mean for the world that language itself is possible.

> Instead of a certain number of predicates being excluded from a thing in virtue of the identity of its concept, each 'thing' opens itself up to the infinity of predicates through which it passes [. . .] The communication of events replaces the exclusion of predicates. (Deleuze 1990: 174)

In contrast to those who try to explain how the world falls under a concept or predicate (Frege) or lies outside of the realm of signification (Saussure), Deleuze views language as a matter of communication; more precisely, the communication of events. Such communication is not, as yet, language. It involves the mixing and mingling of entities that cannot yet be said to be individuals, to be possible objects of perception or knowledge (see Deleuze 1990: 4–5, 21). The infinity of possible events is thus characterised by an infinity of predicates, rather than viewing a set of predicates or signs as primary, and to which the world is supposed to conform.

Deleuze's approach is speculative, in the positive sense of the term (as discussed in Chapter 1, with regard to the work of Whitehead (1978) and Stengers (2011; 2014)).[3] That is to say, his ideas offer an alternative rendition of the questions and problems that have arisen in thinking about the world and language, and their interrelation. Deleuze is well aware of those attempts to render such relations in terms of logic and signification, but he finds them lacking (Deleuze 1990: 12–19). His aim is to rethink the heart of the matter by focusing on neglected aspects, such as the relation between verbs and infinity. Deleuze's ideas are not intended to produce a more accurate 'picture' of the world, but seek to develop a new approach to the problems that we have inherited. To demand that philosophy provide a picture of the world is already to accept the claim that there is a reality to be pictured. Early on in *The Logic of Sense* Deleuze talks of 'an economic or strategic question' (1990: 17). It is not primarily a question of whether verbs 'really are' infinite but of whether this approach produces new and productive avenues of thought. The adequacy of his concepts is to be judged in the extent to which he enables some of the knots that inhibited previous theories to be avoided.

It is in these terms that Deleuze states that events have interrelations that comprise part of what makes language possible. And, as Deleuze and Guattari comment regarding the work of Whitehead: 'Interaction becomes *communication*' (Deleuze

---

3. See Halewood (2017) for a discussion of some of the pitfalls and benefits of speculation in contemporary thought.

and Guattari 1994: 154). Language bears witness to, and is an example of, the inherent activity and interactivity that is more fundamental than the appearance of individual acts or actions; it is this which is expressed in the infinitive form of verbs, which themselves are both implicated in, and an outcome of, such wider processes. Language is not an exception. Deleuze considers verbs to *express* an integral part of existence, one that is not founded upon humans, upon human communication or language, but that human language and communication characterise.

The word 'express' will do quite a lot of conceptual work in the pages that follow. It is envisaged as having a range of connotations. An expression is a meaningful statement in language; but it also retains elements of its etymology, namely, the notion of pressing or squeezing out. The relation between events and language is one that carries both aspects: the linguistic and the material. Language and the world come to be, and have integral interrelations.

Mountains may seem like static entities, but over many millennia they arise and erode. A painting in a museum may seem like an object for contemplation but it is slowly fading and decaying. That all things are, ultimately, transient is no secret, but such ideas are kept in the background and the world is usually thought of as made up of things (nouns) with their inherent qualities (adjectives). Deleuze wants to disrupt this way of thinking, and the notion of the infinite verb is one way to achieve this. He points to the fact that the world as it is now is only one moment in the existence of the universe. It was different and it will be different. Change and process are integral aspects of the world: language is a part of the world, one that is made up of processes and events.

There are still many questions to be answered. For example, if the world is constantly changing, if it is always in flux, then does this mean that there are no things or objects in the world? Are they merely illusions? Is everything relative and meaningless? Such questions have taken hold of some who call themselves postmodernists; they believe that there are no fixed grounds for reality, morality, or thinking. This is not a position adopted by most process philosophers, and certainly not by Deleuze, as will be seen in the next section.

Verbs in the World

So far this chapter has focused on the 'infinite' aspect of verbs. In their infinitive form, verbs do not refer to the action of an individual at a specific time, on a specific occasion. The infinitive form of the verb taps into the limitless potentiality of existence. But the world we live in is not one of infinite possibilities and we are not lost amid continual flows where nothing actually happens. Instead, we find ourselves coming up against real things with real consequences. What has happened before, what is happening now, and what has the potential to happen all act as constraints; such events need to be taken into account. For example, it is difficult to get up in the morning after working late; it is cold outside so the car will not start; the water main has burst so there is a traffic jam, and so on. We wake, we eat, we repair, we wait. These are real occasions and real activities and it certainly will not feel that these are examples of being in touch with an infinite realm of possibility or potentiality. Something is happening, and it is happening now. Deleuze would describe this in terms of the verb having shifted from the infinite to being 'actualised', a shift from the realm of infinite potential to the world of actual happenings. This is the world of the present where people, things and situations appear and interact and the present is replete with constraints. It would be going too far to say that it is language that acts as the only constraint, but the constraints that are encountered in the world can be expressed through language. Indeed, in so far as language is an aspect of the events of the world, 'It is language which fixes the limits' (Deleuze 1990: 2). At the same time, language also keeps in touch with the infinite, with the unbridled process of becoming: 'it is language as well which transcends the limits and restores

them to the infinite equivalence of an unlimited becoming'
(Deleuze 1990: 3).

This tension between language as fixing the limits and yet
being in touch with the infinite is analogous to the tension
between language as seemingly capable of conveying the deepest
desires, feelings or needs of individual humans and language
as an anonymous system that pre-exists and moulds human
thought and desire. This tension was taken up in the twentieth
century by a range of thinkers, especially those working within
the psychoanalytic tradition, for example Jacques Lacan. One
aspect of this tension is that language appears to be both individual and social. Language seems to enable individuals to state
what they feel, want, believe or think, but language also relies
on the majority of the speakers of that language recognising, or
agreeing upon, the words and phrases of the language. Language
is, in this sense, 'social'; it was created by 'other people' prior to
any individual enunciation. It is not possible to pick and choose
the meanings of specific words, contrary to what Lewis Carroll,
in his book *Through the Looking-Glass*, has one of his characters
assert: "'When *I* use a word," Humpty Dumpty said, in rather a
scornful tone, "it means just what I choose it to mean – neither
more nor less."' If individuals assigned their own meanings to
words, then communication would be difficult, if not impossible. Communication relies upon interactions that are prior to
the linguistic. Nevertheless, if language were only some kind
of pre-existing societal system, then would it be possible for
individuals to fully express themselves, to say what they mean?[4]
Setting up the problem in this way, making a division between
language as a social system and language as the method through
which individuals say what they mean, is an example of what
has come to be known as the 'structure–agency' debate. This is a
problem that has dogged social theory throughout the twentieth
century. It suggests that there are two irreconcilable positions:
one emphasises the rigid structure of language, which limits what

---

4. I will return to some (gendered) aspects of this problem in Chapter 7.

we can say; the other emphasises the supposed inventiveness of individual speakers and the way in which they use language to communicate their very specific thoughts and beliefs.

The structure–agency debate is another instance of Whitehead's notion of bifurcation. If language-as-structure is taken as primary, then it becomes the 'real reality', and the individual instances of language as produced by specific speakers are epiphenomena, as they are outcomes of this more basic structural reality. If individual utterances are taken as primary, as the productions of individual intentions or consciousnesses, then the overall system of language becomes an aggregation or reflection of the 'real reality' constituted by these intentions or consciousnesses. One branch of this bifurcation always takes precedence and leads to the same kinds of questions and problems always being generated. While some, such as Giddens (1984) and Stones (2005), have tried to reduce such problems by merging aspects of both sides of the bifurcation through the theory of 'structuration', this would not be the approach that Whitehead would advocate. He would argue that there is a need to recognise that which led to the question being stated in this oppositional way (structure vs agency, or agency vs structure) and to try to reformulate the problem in a new way, in terms of a contrast where the 'inhibitions of opposites have been adjusted into the contrasts of opposites' (Whitehead 1978: 109). This is not to deny the force of the problem or question, but to reorient it. And this is what Deleuze is attempting in his considerations of the relation of the infinite verb to its actualisations in the present.

Deleuze clarifies his argument by building on the work of Foucault (Deleuze 1988). In doing so, Deleuze employs the term 'statements' to describe the *contrast* between the infinite aspect of the verb and the present world in which we find ourselves. 'No sense of possibility or potentiality exists in the realm of statements. Everything in them is real and all reality is manifestly present' (Deleuze 1988: 3). Statements are not produced by individual speakers or subjects; they do not harbour the intentionality of individual humans; 'no originality is needed in order to produce them' (Deleuze 1988: 3). On Deleuze's reading, statements delimit the utter facticity of the moment within which subjects find their place; they are, in this sense, social insofar as they substantiate the actual conditions and consequences of the contemporary world. As Ansell-Pearson puts it, such statements refer not to the verbal utterances of humans but to 'a "language-being" that enjoys its own independent existence, and which produces subjects and objects for themselves as so many immanent variables' (Ansell-Pearson 1999: 132). This is a further contrast, one that does not deface the problem that instantiated the structure–agency debate, but that shifts the ground from which it is produced. Whitehead makes the point as follows: 'subject and object are relative terms' (Whitehead 1933: 226). It is not that subjects and objects are 'unreal' or that they dissolve into some endless becoming. Nor are they manifestations of deeper structures, be these some kind of societal forces or individual consciousnesses. Rather, subjects and objects occur occasionally and always in relationship to each other, in specific instances or events.

Deleuze (1988) also uses the term 'statement' to portray Foucault's texts (1967; 1970; 1972; 1976; 1984; 1991) as a range of attempts to excavate the ways in which language and the world come together both to limit what can be said, what can be done, but also to point to how things could potentially be done or said differently; thereby balancing the infinite and actual aspects of the verbal form. The contingency, which is expressed in the infinite form of verbs, is where that which was raised by the problem of agency resides. Statements can be considered as examples of how language operates in the present as a way of expressing the limits of the world that we find ourselves in. Statements are actualisations of the infinite element of the verb that are rendered in the present. In this way, statements rid the infinite verb of its potentiality or possibility.

> Any institution implies the existence of statements such as a constitution, a charter, contracts, registrations and enrolments. Conversely, statements refer back to an institutional milieu which is necessary for the formation both of the objects which

arise in such examples of the statements and of the subject who speaks from this position (for example the position of the writer in society, the position of the doctor in the hospital or at his [*sic*] surgery), in any given period together with the new emergence of objects. (Deleuze 1988: 9)

'Institutions' refers to those elements that might normally be considered to be social or societal (see Halewood 2012; 2014: 61–90, for a discussion of the important difference between these terms). 'Subject' refers to what might normally be thought of as indicating the individual. Statements lie in between these, but are not a mixing of elements of the social or the individual. All institutions rely on certain statements; the institution of medicine in the UK relies on the notion that doctors should not cause harm to their patients. Institutions, subjects and statements coalesce to constitute a realm of action and speaking within which doctors exercise certain powers and take on specific responsibilities (diagnosing, prescribing, operating). Statements are not purely linguistic. They are tied up with the practices, techniques, tactics, clothing, instruments, pills, potions, buildings, etc. which go to make up what is now considered to be the institution of medicine, with all its hospitals, patients, drugs, doctors, nurses, surgeries, stethoscopes, and so on. In this way, these statements also help create the kinds of individuals or subjects that are to be found within these institutions. Hence Deleuze mentions 'the subject who speaks from this position'. It is not what an individual doctor actually says that matters, at this point. It is what they are able to say and the consequences that this has that matter.

For Deleuze, actualisation is never a complete rendering of potentiality, or of what is possible. The aim is not to solve the structure–agency problem by giving equal weight to both sides, or to merge their functions. While it might appear that Deleuze has focused on the structural aspect, he has, rather, adjusted the conditions of the problem, through his contrast between the infinitive and present, as expressed in different verbal forms. This is not to be balanced by a discussion of the subject or agent and their

61

role within this, as this would fall back into the structure–agency debate, another bifurcation. Instead, Deleuze (and Whitehead) draw out the implications of a specific contrast so that the world is neither purely individual nor social: 'actualization is always both collective and individual, internal and external' (Deleuze 1990: 110). Language is not simply the creation of individual humans or a system into which humans have to fit themselves. To return to the questions raised in previous chapters, language is not simply a reflection of the world; we should not ask how language refers to or grasps the world. Language is a part of the world. There is both the infinite side to this and the actual side. As Deleuze puts it, rather eloquently, in his book on Foucault: 'they [hospitals] are not just figures of stone, assemblages of things [. . .] but first and foremost forms of light that distribute light and dark, opaque and transparent, seen and non-seen, etc.' (Deleuze 1988: 57).

Process, which Deleuze might characterise as the move from the virtual to the actual,[5] never exhausts the novelty, force or power that characterise its implication in the contemporary world. Over and beyond immediate actualisations of events in contemporary bodies, there remains the force of the eventfulness of the universe that enables the future and the past in distinction to the present.

> There is also another movement wherein the event implies something excessive in relation to its actualization, something that overthrows worlds, individuals and persons, and leaves them to the depth of the ground which works and dissolves them. (Deleuze 1990: 167–8)

It is for this reason that Deleuze and Whitehead insist that to view language as the designator of an external reality is to misrecognise the complexity of the interrelation of events, things, language and the world. For, 'the predication of properties veils radically different relations between entities' (Whitehead 1964:

---

5. See, for example, Deleuze (1993: 79).

19). Deleuze takes this further: 'The world is predication itself, *manners* being the particular predicates, and the subject, what goes from one predicate to another as if from one aspect of the world to another' (Deleuze 1993: 53, emphasis added). The next chapter will analyse the role of such 'manners' through a discussion of the importance of adverbs in the work of John Dewey, and the importance not just of what happens but *how* it happens. Before turning to this, one final element of Deleuze's thought will be considered – the construction of sense.

Making Sense

As was seen in previous chapters, Frege, Russell and Saussure started from the supposition that language could make sense on its own terms, and that its relation to the world came later. Deleuze asks a more fundamental question, namely what does it mean to '*make* sense'. Importantly, this is not simply to do with one individual making sense of the words of another. Deleuze argues that sense is created, fabricated even, taking the broader view that the world, somehow, enables sense to be made (which ultimately allows for us to make sense of the world). In doing so, Deleuze does not dismiss those elements that have attracted the attention of other writers, such as Frege, Russell and Saussure. 'Many authors agree in recognizing three distinct relations within the proposition' (Deleuze 1990: 12). As a result, Deleuze pays due attention to the role of 'denotation' (as in the work of Frege and Russell), 'signification' (as in the work of Saussure) and 'manifestation'.[6] It is not that Deleuze believes these relations to be fictitious or fallacious; rather, 'From denotation to manifestation, then to signification, but also from signification

---

6. To put it briefly, by 'manifestation', Deleuze means the way in which an individual speaker can legitimately be said to 'mean what they say'. I have not discussed the question of 'intention' with regard to language in this book. It is an interesting area; however, it is not directly relevant to

to manifestation and to denotation, we are carried along a circle, which is the circle of the proposition' (Deleuze 1990: 16–17). Analyses of language have tended to maintain that the proposition contained within sentences is self-sufficient. Denotation is solely concerned with the truth or falsehood of propositions. Manifestation 'concerns the relation of the proposition to the person who speaks and expresses himself' (Deleuze 1990: 13). Signification 'consider[s] the elements of the proposition as "signifying" conceptual implications capable of referring to other propositions' (Deleuze 1990: 14).

Deleuze maintains that none of these terms fully explains what is meant by the sense of a proposition, and, more importantly, *how* a proposition makes sense. Deleuze argues that there must be a fourth relation of the proposition, one beyond denotation, manifestation and signification. This fourth relation is 'sense'.

> Sense is the fourth dimension of the proposition. The Stoics discovered it along with the event: sense: *the expressed of the proposition*, is an incorporeal, complex and irreducible entity, at the surface of things, a pure event which inheres or subsists in the proposition. (Deleuze 1990: 19, emphasis in original)

Sense is 'the expressed of the proposition'. It is not merely what the proposition expresses; indeed, it is not limited to the proposition. If it were, then sense would remain within the circle of the proposition and would have to be explained in terms of denotation, manifestation or signification. At the same time, sense is not a simple property of things as they are. Furthermore, sense is not reducible to the perceptions or judgements of subjects confronted either by propositions or things. Sense as 'that which is expressed by the proposition . . . [is] irreducible to individual states of affairs, particular images, personal beliefs, and universal or general concepts' (Deleuze 1990: 19).

---

my argument here. Some of the most important writers in this field are the later Wittgenstein, especially in *Philosophical Investigations*; J. L. Austin (1911–60) and his book *How to Do Things With Words*; and John Searle (1932–) and his book *Speech Acts*.

To give an example: if someone were sitting with a glass of wine and said: 'My glass is half full', then this seems to 'make sense'. Clearly something in the world is indicated or denoted by what was said, namely, a glass and the wine it contains. But this would also have been indicated if the speaker had stated that 'My glass is half empty.' The denotation of the glass and the wine do not fully characterise the situation. Also, it is evident that the speaker is trying to communicate a specific concept that they hope the hearer will understand – they are being optimistic. This is what is signified by the original statement. Such signification may convey the meaning of the sentence, but does it explain *how* the phrase makes sense? Finally, it could be argued that this sentence only makes sense because it somehow articulates the thoughts or state of mind of the speaker, their intention (this invokes the notion of manifestation). It may well be the case that this statement is linked to that individual's state of mind, but this is not the only reason why the statement makes sense. If it had been spoken by someone else, or was to be found in a novel, it would still make sense. So, Deleuze argues, sense must be located somewhere else. That is to say, over and beyond all of these aspects of intentional meaning, signifying and pointing to the world, there is something that enables the statement to make sense. According to Deleuze, sense involves the very possibility that something is expressed by the sentence.[7] This something is not a thing or object in the world but is the very *activity* of expression.

Deleuze then comments on the complexity of this notion. 'It is difficult to respond to those who wish to be satisfied with

---

7. Intriguingly, Frege also moves towards a similar notion of sense as something that exists beyond individual statements or propositions and that has its own kind of existence. He makes such points most clearly in his essay 'Sense and Meaning' which can be found in the collection of his essays *Translations from the Philosophical Writings of Gottlob Frege* (Frege 1980). Here he attempts to link sense to what is expressed by a proposition. There is much of interest here. But he differs from Deleuze, and I would say falls short of him, in that he ultimately ties sense back to the logical form of language and not to the activity of the world itself.

words, things, images and ideas' (Deleuze 1990: 20). One reason for this is the prevalence of the concept of a bifurcated world, where existence is sorted into two different camps. On this occasion there are, it seems, the real things (or objects) that are external to human subjects. In the other camp lie the words used by such subjects to describe the things of the world; a realm constituted by the ideas and images that are formed of such things, but that themselves are separate from the world. This way of dividing up the world is so ingrained that it is difficult to imagine that there may be more than just words and things. It is precisely this 'more than' which Deleuze is trying to invoke when he talks about 'sense'.

Sense does not 'exist', with regard to Deleuze's understanding of the conditions of existence. 'For we may not even say that sense exists either in things or in the mind; it has neither physical nor mental existence' (Deleuze 1990: 20). Moreover, sense is something that cannot be grasped nor can it be named as such: 'we can only infer it indirectly' (Deleuze 1990: 20). Sense is that which accompanies an event, in that it describes not how the subject makes sense of the world but how the world *makes* sense, creates sense, constructs sense, is both language-like and material, thereby enabling the later instances of denotation, signification, manifestation. Sense is expressed, is squeezed out. It is this prior process of making sense that enables the creation and completion of subjects and individuals.

> Sense is both the expressible or the expressed of the proposition, and the attribute of the state of affairs. It turns one side towards things and one side towards propositions. But it does not merge with the propositions which it expresses any more than with the state of affairs or the quality which the proposition denotes. (Deleuze 1990: 22, emphasis in original)

There is no need to separate language from the world; the fundamental question is not that of how language refers to, or grasps, the things of the world. For language, in terms of its propositions, is a part of the world. This is because sense is both part of

66

such propositions and part of the world, considered as a state of affairs rather than an enduring, underlying, substantial entity (as Aristotle would have it).

Conclusion

Language does not represent, reflect or create the world. Events or states of affairs make language possible. Language does not make (create) sense on its own terms; it is only one element in the wider process of ongoing existence. Yet sense is not a simple property of things as they are. Nor is sense reducible to the perceptions or judgements of individual humans. It is not that Deleuze believes that language is the cornerstone of existence but, rather, that the activity of the world is expressed through the notion of the verb. It is the activity of the world that *makes* (creates) sense. This is why the notion of static things or nouns with their changeable properties (adjectives) is inadequate to describe the world. The world is not made up of words and things but of events. For example, we tend to think that most trees are green (at some point in the year, at least) and might state that 'trees are green'. This approach treats trees as static objects that have certain fixed properties. In such a model, trees are seen as passive things that are perceived or talked about by active humans who are independent of such trees. It is an example of Aristotle's subject–predicate approach, and is tied to his assertion of a 'primary substance'. Deleuze offers an alternative approach, one that views the world as in process, as ongoing, as an active place. Rather than say 'The tree is green', he tries to describe the activity of the tree's being green. This is the crucial role of verbs. "'*The tree greens*'" – is this not finally the sense of the color of the tree; and is not "*the tree greens*" its global meaning?' (Deleuze 1990: 21). And, by corollary, as Whitehead puts it: 'We enjoy the green foliage of the spring greenly' (Whitehead 1933: 321).

There is a need to go beyond the apparent form of our sentences, not to uncover their logical form or to identify the system of signification that lies below, but to change the mode in which we understand both language and the world. This is one role of both philosophy and poetry for, as Whitehead puts it: 'Philosophy is *akin* to poetry [. . .] In each case there is reference to form beyond the direct meanings of words' (Whitehead 1938: 237–8, emphasis added). Texts such as Wallace Stevens's *The Man with the Blue Guitar* can help us think about questions of process, of colours, of the world, for example when he writes: 'Slowly the ivy on the stones/ Becomes the stones' (Stevens 1984: 170–1). Moreover, Stevens's poem, concerned as it is with 'describing' a painting by Picasso (*The Old Guitarist*), is immersed in questions of both colour and music as integral to the existence of the painting and the poem itself, without being fixed in the world (as nouns) or mere products of our experience or reading of the poem or painting: 'sun's green, / Cloud's red, earth feeling, sky that thinks?' (Stevens 1984: 177). Instead, there is a need to consider and reform our language, to allow for the becoming of the colours and the poem itself: 'The man bent over his guitar / A shearsman of sorts. The day was green. / They said, "You have a blue guitar, / You do not play things as they are." / The man replied, "Things as they are / Are changed upon the blue guitar"' (Stevens 1984: 165). Accounting for reality and change is the remit of both philosophy and poetry, in their different manners; that is why they are '*akin*', rather than identical.

It is important that any such renewed understanding is not limited solely to the realm of thought. As has been seen, Deleuze is not simply proposing a new way of thinking about language, the world, or their interrelation. If this were the case, then he would fall back into the trap of correlationism, as his theory would be grounded only in the realm of thinking about the world, without direct access to the world itself. The correlationist circle would not have been broken, merely presented in a different light. Likewise, if Deleuze's position were merely an emanation of human thought or consciousness, it would reinforce the bifurcation of nature. Human cognition would be set up as a primary realm of activity, which is distinct from a passive world that takes no part in the operations of consciousness. This is one reason why Deleuze is impatient with those 'who wish to be satisfied with words, things, images and ideas'. For such wishes limit the kind of questions that can be asked, with the result that the answers to such questions will endlessly repeat both the correlationist circle and other insidious bifurcations.

In light of this, I would suggest that what Deleuze offers is a novel attitude towards language and the world, in the sense of a novel mode of paying attention to their status and inter-relation. It is also an attitude *within* language and the world. This attitude incorporates that which is usually rendered in terms of cognition, thought or consciousness but also includes more. Quite what comprises this 'more' will be taken up in the next two chapters. Two key elements will be discussed. First, an insistence that 'how' things happen is integral to all items and occasions of existence. This entails that thought, too, is an occasion within the world and, therefore, always happens in a certain manner. There is a 'how' to thinking. Second, thought is not dislocated from the body. This is not to invoke some kind of physical or biological body as the generative locus of thought. To prioritise either the body or thought is, once again, to assert a bifurcation. Chapter 6 will outline Whitehead's notion of 'bodilyness', and its relation to prepositions and symbolism, in order to explain how a contrastive interweaving of those elements that are usually separated into two separate arenas – thought and the body – enables both the bifurcation of nature and the correlationist circle to be avoided.

With regard to the status of language, this may mean rele-gating the importance of adjectives, or at least recognising that they only give a partial perspective. 'Greenness' is not a temporary property or attribute of static things; it expresses an active element that expresses ongoing existence, the process of a tree, for example. It gains its purchase from the verb 'to green', rather than picking out a fixed quality that is then assigned to the supposedly passive or neutral tree. Instead, language expresses 'a "manner of being" of the thing, an "aspect" that exceeded the

Aristotelian alternative, essence–accident' (Deleuze 1993: 53). The importance of the notion of a 'manner of being' will be taken up in the next chapter. The world is not made up of objects and subjects that have their own specific kind of effects. Indeed, effects 'are not physical qualities and properties [. . .] They are not things or facts, but events [. . .] They are not substantives or adjectives but verbs' (Deleuze 1990: 4–5). Deleuze, therefore, develops an attitude towards the importance of happenings, events and verbs that express the interrelations of language and the world. To develop such an attitude, it is necessary to consider not just happenings and events but *how* such events occur. It is, therefore, time to turn to the status and role of adverbs.

5

Adverbs: Dewey on the Qualities of Existence

The preceding chapter presented Deleuze's discussion of verbs both as expressing the potentiality of existence (in the infinitive mode) and as inhering in the contemporary world (in the present tense). This chapter argues that John Dewey (1859–1952) likewise develops a philosophical approach that avoids thinking in terms of nouns and adjectives, in terms of objects and their properties. Dewey focuses on *how* things are done. This links to what Deleuze called the 'manner of being'. It is a mistake to build a gap between human experience (or language) and the world. Not only is activity inherent to the world, but the manner in which such activity occurs needs to be understood, as this too is integral to the world, not an addition to the world. Things always happen in a certain way: quality suffuses existence. For Dewey, such qualities are best described through adverbs which convey the manner of such activity. Adverbs relate when and, more importantly, *how* things happen. They are linked to verbs and add to them by modifying them. We eat well or badly; we drive slowly or recklessly; the plant grows quickly or poorly. Things never simply eat, drive or grow.

An important element of Dewey's thought is his notion of 'possession'. For Dewey, possession is not about ownership; it is not a question of one thing having, grasping or capturing another. Words do not grasp or possess the world or, to put it another way, the mind does not gain possession of the world through knowing the meaning of certain words. Rather, existence is the coming together of living things and some part of the world into an *active* experience. Existence is a form of co-belonging.[1]

Dewey on Possession and Knowledge

The word 'possession' carries a range of meanings. In the active sense, as a verb, 'to possess' implies the ownership of something by another individual (or subject). Taken as a noun, possession suggests the thing that is owned. A third meaning reverses the polarity of the first and describes the taking over of an individual by some external force – when a person is possessed by jealousy or demons, or a crowd is possessed by anger. These shades of meaning of the word 'possession' suggest a background view of existence that is populated by subjects (humans) and objects. Dewey, however, refuses any sharp division of the world that presupposes a split between such subjects and objects, a gap between nature and society, between language and the world. He does not allow nature to bifurcate. Instead, he both starts and ends with experience, without premising such experience on humans or on human experience.

Dewey maintains that traditional models of knowledge imply a form of possession as ownership; ownership of the world. 'Greek thought regarded possession [. . .] as the essence of science, and thought of the latter as [. . .] a complete possession of reality' (Dewey 1958: 134). This is a view that still haunts science, philosophy and everyday thought. Such a concept of possession is also reflected in phrases such as 'having an idea' or 'having a feeling', for example. Words appear to enable us to possess (knowledge of) the world. To know something is to have it for oneself, to possess the truth or essence of what is known.

---

1. It should be noted that the term 'co-belonging' is not one that Dewey uses himself. I have adopted it to point up and emphasise the particular and productive aspects of Dewey's account of existence and possession, aspects that might otherwise be skimmed over or missed.

This is more than a psychological state of certainty; when something is known it appears to confer the ability and right to manipulate it. Once it is known that gold is soluble in a mixture of water and cyanide then it is possible to extract gold from a range of ores. Knowledge of what makes someone commit a crime implies the possibility of intervening and altering the behaviour of that person. Knowledge considered as possession also presupposes a gap between the knower and what is known, the 'owner' of the knowledge and the object of the knowledge. Our language is a crucial part of such knowledge and possession. Or so it is supposed.

Furthermore, philosophy has also tended to describe the world as 'given' either to the human subject, to perception, to thought or to consciousness. Such a model entails a primary division between an external 'reality' and the inner operations of the human mind that knows this 'reality' (or fails to know it). The way in which the world has been given to humans has long been a matter of dispute. As discussed in Chapters 2 and 3, the problem initially involved questions about whether properties belong to the world, or to the subject that perceives the world. More recently, these debates have shifted to questions about consciousness and language. Still, the parameters remain the same. Words capture the sense of things, if not things in themselves.

According to Dewey, to approach the question in this way is mistaken: 'There is nothing in nature that *belongs* absolutely and exclusively to anything else; belonging is always a matter of reference and distributive assignment, justified in any particular case as far as it works out well' (Dewey 1958: 234, emphasis in original). The notion of possession, conceived in terms of ownership, assumes that objects and subjects are separate; this separation is found in Greek philosophy but not in existence. Of course, entities can be described as objects and subjects, but these descriptions are not indicative of what things and events are really like in themselves. Objects and subjects are elements of a wider complex of activity, one that is made up of what Dewey terms 'undergoings', 'doings', 'beginnings', 'endings'. Although

Dewey has chosen a range of nouns to make his point, it should be noted that these are slightly unusual nouns that retain the activity expressed by verbs. These specific nouns take on the role of expressing that the world is not static but 'eventful'. Although Dewey does not use the word 'event' as a technical aspect of his philosophy, it is possible to read his characterisation of existence in terms of 'undergoings', 'doings', 'beginnings', 'endings' as indicating a similar train of thought to that of Deleuze. As will be seen below, a fuller description of such eventfulness requires the addition of adverbs, of the adverbial.

Experience is Real

In order to avoid the traditional separation of subjects and objects, of language and the world, Dewey situates experience as the cornerstone of his philosophy. It is important to approach this idea with care. Usually experience is taken to be private, as something that belongs to an individual, making it difficult not to think of experience in terms of something that happens to, or *belongs* to, a person. Dewey makes his point in as follows:

> [The] implication is that experience by its very nature is owned by some one; and [. . .] that everything about experience is affected by a private and exclusive quality. The implication is as absurd as it would be to infer from the fact that houses are usually owned, are mine and yours and his [*sic*], that possess-ive reference so permeates the properties of being a house that nothing intelligible can be said about the latter. (Dewey 1958: 231–2)

Dewey believes that it is possible to think of experience without always invoking an individual human subject who does the experiencing. This enables him to avoid having to describe experience as something that always involves possession. If experience is seen as only involving humans, this raises the question of how experience can be rejoined with the world that is being experienced. Here lie the pitfalls of secondary qualities and correlationism, as outlined in Chapter 3. If words only refer to what humans think or feel about things, then it is hard to see how the gap between such experiences, or words, and the things of the world can be bridged. Dewey avoids such a gap by describing human experience (and language) as immersed in the world, as an aspect of the world. He holds that human 'selves' occur within a wider milieu of experiences, which they do not simply create or own. '*Among and within*[2] these occurrences, not outside of them nor underlying them, are those events which are denominated selves' (Dewey 1958: 232, emphasis added).

This implies that experience is itself 'real', and not derived from or dependent upon a self or an individual human.

> Experience when it happens has the same dependence upon objective natural events, physical and social, as has the occurrence of a house. It has its own objective and definitive traits; these can be described without reference to a self, precisely as a house is of brick, has eight rooms, etc., irrespective of whom it belongs to. (Dewey 1958: 232)

Experience is located *in* the world. This does not mean that Dewey views experience as an independent entity that has its own existence, external to humans, waiting to be picked up and carried by individuals. This would run the risk of treating experience as simply another object that can be known by science or philosophy. It would replicate the original problem and bring in the notion of possession again, through the back door. Dewey's position may appear to occupy a middle ground but it is no tepid compromise; it is a radical philosophical gesture. The 'reality' of experience lies in both object and subject; the human individual and the world; in what is experienced and how it is experienced. In this sense:

---

2. Importantly, 'among' and 'within' are both prepositions, although Dewey does not comment on this. The next chapter will draw out the role that prepositions play in language and the world.

experience is *of* as well as *in* nature. It is not experience which is experienced but nature – stones, plants, animals, diseases, health, temperature, electricity, and so on. Things interacting in certain ways *are* experience; they are what is experienced [. . .] they are *how* things are experienced as well. (Dewey 1958: 4a, emphases in original)

Experience is not just 'out there' waiting to be felt. Experience is the process and manner of feeling the world; a specific world made up of cars, dogs, lies, failures, identity cards, magic tricks and whistles. Crucially, these are always experienced in a certain way; *excitedly, patiently, resignedly, amazedly* – adverbially. Adverbs are not just human additions to, or descriptions of, existence. Just as Deleuze insisted that verbs express something of the world, Dewey outlines how the adverbial expresses a key aspect of existence.

To recap: Dewey invites us to move beyond a simple model of possession where one thing owns or is given to another. He develops a position that aims to avoid thinking and acting in terms of nouns by learning to accept the world in terms of its qualities, qualifiers and qualifications (Dewey 1958: 75, 318; 2005: 222–3). Philosophy should discard its obsession with nouns and their adjectival properties. The real task is to describe the activities of existence and how these are modified. Adverbs express the urgency and importance of existence. 'I don't just want the money or contract or reassurance – I need the money or contract or reassurance *urgently*. I need it *now*.' Adverbs, and an adverbial slant to thought, enable a move beyond the limited facts of existence, which nouns claim to describe, and begin to elaborate the manner, meaning and import of experience and existence. '"Thought," reason, intelligence, whatever word we choose to use, is existentially an adjective (or better an adverb), not a noun. It is a disposition of activity' (Dewey 1958: 158).

Dewey further explains this interrelation between experience, experiencer and the quality of experience through a discussion of sound: 'sounds *come* from outside the body, but sound itself is near, intimate; it is an excitation of the organism; we feel the

76

clash of vibrations throughout our whole body' (Dewey 2005: 246, emphasis in original). Where is the sound? It is both out there and in us. The car crashes and we jump because we hear it. The sound is part of the same event that is made up of the car crashing and us jumping. Moreover, all sounds have some quality. 'A sound is itself threatening, whining, soothing, depressing, fierce, tender, soporific, in its own quality' (Dewey 2005: 247). Every sound is different. This difference comes from its quality. Violins and crying babies create different sounds, even when they are of the same frequency or pitch. There is no such thing as the pure sound of the violin; there are only ever the different qualities of sound of different violins. It may be technically possible to separate sound from its immediate qualities, to measure its frequency and compare it to the frequencies generated by other objects, but, in doing so, such sounds are artificially separated from what they actually *are* on specific occasions. In this way, Dewey rebuts the approach of psychologists such as Levitin (2006) who maintain that music is some kind of 'perceptual illusion' imposed by the brain upon the objective sounds of the world. Sounds and adverbs are intertwined. Violins play *warmly*, *loudly*, for example. This quality of all existence, which is expressed adverbially, indicates that there is nothing that simply happens: things, events, occasions always occur in a certain way. As Whitehead puts it: '*how* an actual entity *becomes* constitutes *what* that actual entity *is*' (Whitehead 1978: 23, emphases in original). This statement comes in Whitehead's major metaphysical treatise *Process and Reality*. Although Dewey's texts are not as avowedly metaphysical, they do contain a metaphysical outlook, one that provides a novel conception of the nature of Nature.

The Qualities of Nature

To state that qualities exist, that they are *in* nature, does not mean that they are 'natural' in the sense of being unchangeable, preordained and outside the influence of individual humans or other acting entities. For Dewey, nature is not opposed to society, and the natural is not opposed to the cultural. Such divisions are produced by an uncritical acceptance of a more fundamental (conceptual) division between what is fixed and what is impermanent. As discussed in Chapter 3, Whitehead argues that this division was generated within Aristotelian philosophy and, despite its outdated premises, is still influential today, and lingers in debates arising from questions surrounding secondary qualities. Dewey places qualities firmly *in* nature and this is why an adverbial philosophy is needed to describe it. 'Nature is kind and hateful, bland and morose, irritating and comforting, long before she [*sic*] is mathematically qualified or even a congeries of "secondary" qualities like colors and their shapes' (Dewey 2005: 15).

Those who argue that qualities are the creations of human attitudes or perceptions run this risk of denying that the world has any qualities. Their position seems to create a different 'reality', one that is generated by human thought alone. This is then separated off from the supposedly more 'real reality' that is studied by science. A geologist may enjoy analysing rocks, may regard them as beautiful, but cannot afford to claim that rocks, in themselves, are enjoyable or beautiful for their own sake – not if the geologist wants to retain their status as a scientist. The human mind alone is taken to produce qualities, values, which are then projected on to the otherwise uninterested and inert objects of the world (this is one important sense of the word 'objective'). Dewey condemns such manoeuvres not simply because they rely on an outdated approach to science and philosophy, but because they dogmatically assume that qualities are unreal, before all the evidence is in. Instead, Dewey declares that qualities inhabit both the world and experiences of the world.

> *Things* are beautiful and ugly, lovely and hateful, dull and illuminated, attractive and repulsive. Stir and thrill in us is as much theirs as is length, breadth, and thickness. Even in the utility of things, their capacity to be employed as means and agencies, is

first of all not a relation, but a quality possessed, immediately possessed. (Dewey 1958: 108–9, emphasis in original)

It is here that the notion of possession returns. Possession now refers to the fact that quality cannot be separated from existence. Moreover, Dewey makes his case not through reference to objects but to things. There are not objects *and* qualities. There are always things with qualities that make those things what they are. This makes the question of possession, as a form of ownership, redundant. Qualities suffuse existence, experience and nature. It is in this sense that nature possesses quality.

This new description of possession conflates all three meanings that were outlined at the start of this chapter. Something in nature exhibits (possesses) a quality. There is also the sense of 'having', in that some entity (often a human) has an experience. Yet the quality of an experience also possesses the experiencer. Possession is a multifaceted aspect of the process of existence which might better be described as a mode of belonging. It is really a matter of '*co*-belonging'. This involves a form of *having* that is distinct from the more dogmatic notion of possession.[3] Co-belonging, for Dewey, marks the coming together of diverse elements such as *this* or *that* experience. Co-belonging also involves both partial possession and being partially possessed. The *manner* in which these two aspects of possession occur provides the third element, the adverbial. Experiences are events in which the different elements and qualities belong together and none of them fully *own* (possess) any of the others. We (on the insistence that such a 'we' includes rocks, cabbages, fun fairs, amoebas, etc.) are changed through the experiences in which we co-belong with other things and qualities. We have things gladly and things have us under sufferance, or equally likely, we have things under sufferance and they have us gladly. Either way, the having always occurs in a specific way, that is, adverbially.

---

3. For a discussion of the philosophical notion of being as 'having', see Debaise (2006: 70–1).

Linking adverbs to the qualities of the world does not entail that such qualities are always good, valuable, or to be strived after for their own sake. 'Qualities have defects as necessary conditions of their excellencies; the instrumentalities of truth are the causes of error; change gives meaning to permanence and recurrence makes novelty possible' (Dewey 1958: 47). Nature should not be envisaged as a unified entity to be known or possessed. Nature, or 'the world', considered as a single entity, does not exist and there is no single purpose, plan or reason for existence. Existence is, in and of itself, incomplete and contradictory. It is not one. If it were, if harmony reigned (as a surprisingly large contingent of philosophers and scientists seem to hold), then there would be no surprises.

> Were there complete harmony in nature, life would be spontaneous efflorescence. If disharmony were not in both man [sic] and nature, if it were only between them, man [sic] would be the ruthless overlord of nature, or its querulous oppressed subject (Dewey 1958: 421)

> nature itself is wistful, pathetic, turbulent and passionate. Were it not, the existence of wants would be a miracle. (Dewey 1958: 64)

The incompleteness of the world allows for action and engagement, for new things to happen, for change to occur. This incompleteness also allows for there to be differences that constitute the world, so that the world is not a unified entity. This is one reason why I have retained the term 'world' as opposed to 'worlds', as the former can still manifest the notion of incompleteness, variety and lack of unity that is suggested by the latter. While Deleuze sees potentiality as suffusing existence through the infinite form of the verb, incompleteness and contingency are integral aspects of Dewey's distinctive concept of nature. Adverbs and an adverbial slant to thinking are required to describe the pathos and joy of existence, as well as the facts of existence.

The Natural vs the Social

Dewey envisages nature as the arena within which all events, objects, qualities and phenomena arise and pass on. The human, the social, the imaginary, the false are not derived from, or pale reflections of, nature. Thinking, imagining and values do not inhabit a separate realm. Dewey's approach is both democratic and demanding. Every *thing* must be granted its rightful claim to existence: trees, thoughts, ships, horses, centaurs, belief in centaurs and bubble-gum. Dewey does not want to grant any special powers to reason and thought that would make them 'supernatural in the literal sense of the word' (Dewey 1958: 265). The assertion that reason and thought are separate from the operations of nature puts thinking above nature, making it, literally, supernatural. Almost paradoxically, this undermines the claims of reason and thought to be active within the world, as they have no rightful or effective place in it, as they are above and outside of nature. As a result, Dewey sets about establishing the placement of qualities, thinking and mind as elements *in* nature. This will involve the refusal of any simple opposition between what is natural and what is social.

> There is a peculiar absurdity in the question of how individuals become social, if the question is taken literally. Human beings illustrate the same traits of immediate uniqueness and connection, relationship, as do other things. (Dewey 1958: 174–5)

This is not to reduce the social to the natural. Dewey is not claiming that nature 'explains' or 'produces' the social in some kind of causal or epiphenomenal way. The social is not distinct from the processes of existence that make up nature.

That which is specific about the social, according to Dewey, is that it is comprises 'uniqueness and connection, relationship'. It is thus a mix of uniqueness *and* relationships *and* connections that constitutes Dewey's very specific concept of sociality, which is itself key to the notion of co-belonging that has been developed in this chapter. Moreover, sociality is a part of nature and helps explain existence as a process in which the elements of the world come together in order to be. 'Association' also becomes a crucial term, as long as it is understood that association is not limited to human societies.[4] 'The catching up of human individuals into association is thus no new and unprecedented fact; it is a manifestation of a commonplace of existence' (Dewey 1958: 175). The social is not a creation of humans. Human society and human language are examples of forms of association, of a coming and holding together, but are not unique. They are examples of that which is to be found throughout existence. It is important not to reimpose already existing categories back on to nature. Dewey is not suggesting that the current concept of human society be taken as paradigmatic, and examples of it be searched for in nature, as some tend to do when trying to understand the so-called societies, or even cultures, of ants, bees and great apes. The challenge is to reconfigure our most basic concept of what constitutes the social.

Returning to the theme of possession: once the notion of ownership is given up, then the 'catching up of human individuals into association' can be seen as a form of possession, in the sense of co-belonging. This makes it easier to understand how humans are seized, infected or *possessed* by ideas, dreams, ideologies. Such seizing marks the adverbial character of existence. This mention of ideology introduces the concept of power, and it is interesting to note that in Foucault's attempts to reconfigure this contentious notion he implicitly agrees with Dewey on the importance of approaching power in terms of its adverbial aspect, by focusing on 'how' it is exercised. This recasting is most evident in Foucault's later works, published in the 1970s, where he makes an analysis of the changing operations of power one of the mainstays of books such as *Discipline and Punish* (1975) and *The History of Sexuality, Volume One* (1976). Foucault does not believe that it is possible to have a theory of power, as power

---

4. This has similarities to Latour's more recent notion of a 'sociology of associations' (see Latour 2005).

is not a 'thing' like other things.[5] The task that he sets himself, especially in his later work, is not to discover what power *is*, but *how* it operates. Foucault argues that 'Power exists only when it is put into action' and makes it clear that he is only interested in 'power relations and not power itself' (1982: 219). This shifts the focus. It is *how* power relations (not power itself) operate in specific places and on specific occasions that is key. According to Foucault, we should not start with 'large-scale' entities such as the state, the police, gender, capitalism and so on, but with 'small-scale' occurrences such as those to be found in the development of the modern prison, hospital, school or military barracks, in order to trace the 'how' of power. The issue of how power operates within specific instances and examples of language will be taken up in Chapters 7 and 8.

Meaning and Language

As is the case with experience and qualities, meanings are not simply created by humans; meaning is to be found in the associations between things and humans. With regard to language, Dewey's interest lies in how meanings can produce actions and reactions. 'The meaning, for example, of portability is something in which two persons and an object share' (Dewey 1958: 187). Language clearly involves humans but does not 'belong' to them alone. Other things, and other entities, are always involved; incorporating, for example, portability, by expressing the activity of being portable, and hence the meaning of portability. Language communicates and expresses meanings but it does not create them out of nothing.

---

5. Foucault made this point very clearly during a conversation with members of the Department of Psychoanalysis at the University of Vincennes in 1997. A transcription of this was published as 'The Confession of the Flesh', which can be found in a collection of Foucault's essays, interviews and conversations entitled *Power/Knowledge*. Foucault states: 'Power in the substantive sense, "*le*" *pouvoir*, doesn't exist' (1980: 198).

The flower pointed to for example, *is* portable; but apart from language portability is a brute contingency waiting for its actualization upon circumstance. But when A counts upon the understanding and cooperation of B, and B responds to the intent of A, the flower *is* contemporaneously portable though not now actually in movement. Its potentiality, or conditioning of consequences, is an immediately recognized and possessed trait; the flower *means* portability instead of simply *being* portable. (Dewey 1958: 180, emphases in original)

Flowers are portable, but until this is realised, agreed upon and acted upon, 'portability' has no meaning. Portability is something that a flower *has* but not in the sense of ownership; it is a trait, a genuine quality. The meaning of portability can be expressed in language, and its meanings can produce or lead to changes in the world: the flower can be picked and given to someone else as a token of affection, or sold, or used to make a dye. This portability does not only affect humans; it is something that could be acted upon by the wind, a horse, or a river in flood. It is not the having of meanings but the taking-up, or acting-with, of meanings that is important. This is very different from viewing properties as being possessed by passive objects; properties that then have to be grasped or known for that object to be known or 'had'. Dewey emphasises ongoing activities: 'a particular act of *taking*, using, responding to, the meanings involved' (Dewey 1958: 331, emphasis in original). The taking of a flower and giving it to a loved one relies on the co-belonging of the flower, its portability, the picker and the loved one. This temporary association might succeed or fail – the lover may use the flower's portability to wear it on their lapel, or they may toss it, dismissively, into the bin.

Dewey's decisive point is that portability is a genuine aspect of the flower, but not in any passive sense. Portability expresses a form of potentiality, which again resonates with Deleuze's position, as opposed to the supposed capacity 'under the right conditions' that Locke assigns to primary and secondary qualities. Portability does not constitute the essence of the flower but it is a real factor in its existence. Meanings are there, in the world, to be acted upon and with. Meaning does not come only from the human system of language, as Saussure maintains, or from the truth or falsehood of statements, as Frege argues. Dewey's argument is more akin to Deleuze's idea that sense needs to be *made*, to be created; not just by people but by people in the world, and the world in people. According to Dewey, meanings put a thing into productive or constraining relations with the other things with which it associates or co-belongs. It is in this strict sense that nature is predominantly 'social', in that it always involves relations between entities. These relations can involve humans, but they do not have to do so. Sociality is not the pre-rogative of humanity (see Halewood 2014 for a fuller discussion).

Meanings can change when new associations are made and unmade. 'Architecture does not add to stone and wood something that does not belong to them, but it does add to them properties and efficacies which they did not possess in their earlier state' (Dewey 1958: 381–2). This is not to say that wood, or the word 'wood', always had a list of latent properties that waited secretly to be discovered by beavers, fire and humans. Rather, when one of these creatures wrests specific pieces of wood from their immediate locale and puts them into new relations elsewhere, from that moment on wood is, and always had been,[6] good for making dams, burning, making houses, ships and tables. The world is not static and its future is not decided or settled; it is in this way that Dewey can be described as a philosopher of process. Process involves an active engagement that adds to the world. Meanings, language and words are part of the world. This also applies to science:

---

6. With regard to whether such traits were always a part of that object, the first reply should be that such questions miss the point; but if an answer is insisted upon, then the next response should be that they 'had always been there', but only once another entity made sense of them in this specific way. As Latour replies, when asked about Pasteur's 'discovery' of microbes: 'After 1864 airborne germs were there all along' (Latour 1999: 173).

when the imagined possibilities were embodied in a new assemblage of natural materials, the steam engine took its place in nature as an object that has the same physical effects as those belonging to any other physical object. (Dewey 2005: 285)

The simplistic division between the natural and the social that bedevils much of contemporary thought is studiously ignored by Dewey. He develops a simpler, more elegant, and much more effective account. The novel sets of relations and associations that are produced throughout existence by all creatures (be they humans, apes, carbon molecules or washing machines) do not suddenly generate unnatural or supernatural phenomena. The steam engine, the machine gun and Barbie dolls are as much an expression of the possibilities of existence as are geysers, spitting cobras and orchids. They are all a part of nature. What is required is an adverbial philosophy to describe the qualities and co-belongings of such a nature, and this is what Dewey offers.

Conclusion – The Importance of 'of'

Possession is not the holding of one thing by another, it is not the having of an object by another object or a human. Some things may claim total rights over another, but they cannot, in reality, fully possess it and exhaust its meanings, even if they destroy it. Possession is, for Dewey, a partaking, an association with, a co-belonging. Co-belonging is not fixed or essential; it is characterised by the small word 'of', which takes on real significance for Dewey. It establishes the links and relations between things and meaning, experiences and qualities. All these may endure but they may also dissolve. 'The ownership of meanings or mind thus vests in nature; meanings are meanings *of*' (Dewey 1958: 288); 'experience is *of* as well as *in* nature' (Dewey 1958: 4a); 'all structure is structure *of* something; anything defined as structure is a character of *events*, not something intrinsic and *per se*' (Dewey 1958: 72); 'Unless macroscopic things are recognized, cells, electrons, logical elements become meaningless. The latter have meaning only as elements *of* (Dewey 1958: 144); 'Childhood is the childhood *of* and *in* a certain serial process of changes which is just what it is, and so is maturity' (Dewey 1958: 275, all emphases in the original).

Dewey's use of the little word 'of' enables him to avoid the seemingly strict divisions that have infected modern thought. 'Of' is a preposition, and the importance of this class of word will be discussed in more detail in the following chapter. In the work of Dewey, the word enables him to develop an adverbial philosophy of experience that bypasses the bifurcation of nature. There are many and varied things, events, qualities and meanings. It is the coming together of these separate elements, their co-belonging, that characterises the process of existence and its shift from the past, through the present, to the future. This coming together is expressed in the often overlooked word 'of'.

Language is, therefore, a crucial element of such processes. The thinking, acting, speaking human gains its individuality from partaking in and of the world, but this also involves and presupposes the world's partaking in the individual human. As Whitehead puts it: 'We are in the world and the world is in us' (Whitehead 1938: 227). In place of a choice between a passive, fateful reception of the world and the loneliness of the individual human responsible for their own choices and situation, Dewey views existence as a partnership where co-belonging takes precedence over possession. As Deleuze made clear, it is not that there is a world made up of things on the one side, with human words for these things on the other. Language, humans and the world are part of a process in which all these elements are partners.

> Natural events – including social habits – originate thoughts and feelings. To say '*I* think, hope and love' is to say in effect that genesis is not the last word; instead of throwing the blame or the credit for the belief, affection and expectation upon nature, one's family, church or state, one declares one's self to be henceforth a partner. (Dewey 1958: 233, emphasis in original)

There is a need to rethink the interrelation of language and the world. Dewey advocates the abandoning of the quest for the possession of the world in terms of knowing it or naming it. Words do not capture things. Words are part of the process of the world; the meaning of words and phrases is both real and changing. They come about in and with the world and us. The best way to describe such eventful processes is by describing how they happen. This is why adverbs are so important. They indicate how something unfolds and makes it what it is. How we read, speak and hear is linked to how we act and live.

Codicil

When quoting from Dewey in this chapter, it has occasionally been necessary to insert the word '*sic*' at those points when he unthinkingly assumed that his discussion was only about, and directed to, men or males. I have also, every so often, used the plural forms of 'they' or 'their' to refer to an individual, which some might argue is not technically correct. The previous paragraph ended with the statement that 'how we read, speak and hear is linked to how we act and live'. Chapter 7 will take up the relations between specific grammatical terms such as personal pronouns and how we view and act in the world after a consideration of the role of prepositions in language and the world.

6

Prepositions: Whitehead on the 'Withness' of the Body

Prepositions indicate relationships between words and between things. They are often concerned with spatial and temporal relations; expressing, for example, that something is 'below', 'in' or 'with'. As discussed in previous chapters, a major trope in Western philosophy and science has been the presumption of existence as comprised of substance (or substances) that manifest certain properties. Nouns are envisaged as best indicating the substantive element, while adjectives have been deployed to describe the (secondary) properties of substance. The work of Deleuze, Dewey and Whitehead has been offered as a means of avoiding such presuppositions through an emphasis on the activity of verbs and the qualities of existence, as expressed through the adverbial. This chapter will further such arguments by turning to another element of language that has not figured in philosophy, namely prepositions. As Whitehead puts it: 'The taint of Aristotelian Logic has thrown the whole emphasis of metaphysical thought upon substantives and adjectives, to the neglect of prepositions' (Whitehead 1933: 356).

For Whitehead, one of the most important prepositions is 'with', and its associated characteristic of 'withness' (Whitehead 1978: 62 and *passim*). 'For instance, we see the contemporary chair, but we see it *with* our eyes; and we touch the contemporary chair, but we touch it *with* our hands' (Whitehead 1978: 62, emphasis in original). This mention of 'eyes' and 'hands' and their importance for sense-perception signals another neglected element in Western philosophy, with its focus on questions of the mind, thought and consciousness, namely the body. Yet in everyday life the existence of our bodies is important, ongoing and unquestioned; as Whitehead jocularly remarks: 'No one ever says, Here am I, and I have brought my body with me' (Whitehead 1938: 156). Nevertheless, the body has been ignored in much of Western philosophy.

Derrida points out that there has long been an 'unspoken' conflation of thought, speech and mind, and, once again, the figure of Aristotle looms large, for it was he who set out that '"spoken words (ta en tē phone) are the symbols of mental experience [. . .] and written words are the symbols of spoken words" [. . .] it is because the voice, producer of *the first symbols*, has a relationship of essential and immediate proximity with the mind' (Derrida 1976: 11, emphasis in original). Spoken words are the intimates of mental experience. Written words are the secondary markers of such mental experience. The voicing of words, the bodily acts of speaking and writing, have not been given their due place. This has led to the presumption that mental experiences, thought and language all inhabit the same plane, which is different in kind to the plane of the body, of bodily experience, of the physical enunciation of words. This is another example of bifurcation, one that permeates philosophy. 'Philosophers have disdained information about the universe obtained through their visceral feelings, and have concentrated on visual feelings' (Whitehead 1978: 121). However, these 'visual feelings' have not been rendered in terms of their bodilyness. The visual, and the scopic, have been given a privileged place in sense-perception and knowledge without situating these within the bodily existence of our eyes. Sight has been 'envisaged' as the primary source of direct and clear information about the world, allowing direct access of the mind to the world, which seems to occur without the intervention of the body.

Whitehead sets out to counter the conflation of speech, thought and mind by making the body, or bodilyness, a fulcrum of both thought and language; and prepositions play a major role: 'We see *with* our eyes; we do not see our eyes' (Whitehead

1938: 156, emphasis added). This emphasis on bodilyness does not lead Whitehead to advocate any version of biological reductionism. He is not suggesting that there is some kind of 'natural' body that lies behind thought, perception and language, either generating or explaining all such phenomena. Whitehead has a rather particular view of the body: 'Our bodies are largely contrivances' (Whitehead 1978: 178–9); 'The body [. . .] is only a peculiarly intimate bit of the world' (Whitehead 1978: 81); 'my hand is part of my body; and my finger nails are part of my body. Also the breath as it passes in and out of my lungs from my mouth and throat fluctuates in its bodily relationship' (Whitehead 1938: 156). This is why the role of prepositions is so important. They express a form of relation between entities, events or phenomena, without presupposing or determining the character of any of these; bodilyness enables prepositions to fulfil their role of making or breaking relations.

The remainder of this chapter will situate Whitehead's account of the 'withness of the body' within philosophical concerns about perception. Whitehead's contention is that there are two forms of perception that need to be given due recognition, namely 'causal efficacy' and 'presentational immediacy'. The body is involved in both forms of perception through 'withness', the prepositional attitude of being 'with'. The interaction of these two forms of perception produces what Whitehead calls 'symbolic reference'. It is at this point that questions of symbolism and language arise. The chapter will conclude by contrasting Whitehead's approach to symbolism to that of C. S. Peirce through a reading of elements of Eduardo Kohn's (2013) use of the latter in his attempt to develop a form of semiosis and anthropology which goes beyond the human.

A Duality of Perception

As mentioned above, Whitehead bemoans that fact that Western philosophy has concentrated on substances (nouns) and their

qualities (adjectives) at the expense of prepositions. For Whitehead, prepositions, such as 'by', 'into', 'through', 'with' express
important aspects of existence. They need to be given their due
place. In his reading of Descartes and Hume, Whitehead points
out that both authors make use of the preposition 'with' as a key
element of their argument. However, they pass over these elements, seemingly not recognising the importance of such terms.
For example:

> [In] the first Meditation he [Descartes] begins by appealing to
> an act of experience – 'I am here, seated by the fire . . .' He
> then associates this act of experience with his body – 'these
> hands and body are mine' [. . .] Notice the peculiarly intimate
> association with immediate experience which Descartes claims
> for his body, an association beyond the mere sense-perception
> of the contemporary world – 'these hands and feet are mine.'
> (Whitehead 1978: 75)

It is a preposition – 'beyond' – that plays a crucial role. Descartes
may end up doubting the information provided by touch,
sight, hearing etc. (arguing, ultimately, that only the experience
of doubting cannot be doubted): this does not, according to
Whitehead, undermine the importance of the original experience of bodilyness – 'beyond the mere sense-perception
of the contemporary world'. That is to say, Descartes may be
correct in arguing that we are liable to see and hear things that
are not really there. However, the starting point of Descartes'
investigation relies upon a recognition of an experience that is
more fundamental than any immediate act of sense-perception,
in terms of sight or touch. Descartes outlines a bodily experience that subtends the immediacy of our sense-perceptions
of the contemporary world. In this instance, it is the feeling that
'these hands and feet are mine'. This is a feeling that precedes
and enables the later, more elaborated, feeling or experience of
seeing or doubting.

   This is the germ of Whitehead's argument that there are two
forms of perception, of which immediate sense-perception is

only one element. Whitehead maintains that philosophers, such as Descartes, have tended to assume that the immediate sensory perception of colours, shapes and sounds is all that is involved in providing information about the world. Whitehead clarifies his position a few pages further on in *Process and Reality*, when he turns to the work of Hume (again mentioning Descartes):

> we refer first to Descartes in Meditation I, 'These hands and this body are mine'; also to Hume in his many assertions of the type, we see with our eyes. Such statements witness to *direct knowledge of the antecedent functioning of the body in sense-perception.* Both agree though Hume more explicitly that sense-perception of the contemporary world is accompanied by perception of the 'withness' of the body. (Whitehead 1978: 81, emphasis added)

In this remarkable passage, Whitehead contends that most philosophers (and scientists) have assumed that there is only one form of perception, namely the immediate data conveyed by sight, touch, taste, smell and hearing. Whitehead refers to this aspect of perception as 'presentational immediacy', which he describes as 'the experience of the immediate world around us, a world decorated by sense-data dependent on the immediate states of relevant parts of our own bodies' (Whitehead 1927a: 14). Or, more prosaically: 'Presentational immediacy is our perception of the contemporary world by means of the senses' (Whitehead 1978: 311). Whitehead is not denying that such information is possible or pertinent. The mistake lies in believing that this is the only form of perception; a mistake that runs throughout much of Western philosophy.

Descartes and Hume seem dimly aware that such presentational immediacy is only part of the story. This is evident in Descartes' phrase 'these hands and this body are mine', and Hume's insistence on the 'withness of the body'. However, they, and most other philosophers, do not follow up such trains of thought, and so it falls to Whitehead to investigate further. What both Descartes and Hume partially recognise, but do not fully admit, is that immediate instances of contemporary sense-perception presuppose, indeed proceed from, the continuing existence of the body. Furthermore, this ongoing bodily existence is not just a prerequisite for contemporary experience, it is *directly known*: there is '*direct knowledge of the antecedent functioning of the body in sense-perception*'. This is a striking appeal to knowledge. It is not based on rationality, consciousness or on data provided by sense-perception. Indeed, the operations of rationality and the production of sense-data rely upon this more fundamental knowledge of the antecedent functioning of the body, which Whitehead names 'causal efficacy'. Causal efficacy is resolutely prepositional in that it is expressed by the 'withness' that draws its capacity from the characteristic of always acting 'with', of delineating the relations between entities. Furthermore: 'It is this withness that makes the body the starting point for our knowledge of the circumambient world. We find here our direct *knowledge* of "causal efficacy"' (Whitehead 1978: 81, emphasis added). This is a striking use of the word 'knowledge'. It is a knowledge of the body by the body. It is genuine knowledge but is prior to the more usual accounts of knowledge that rely on notions of rationality, thought and the mind. Indeed, such 'rational' knowledge presupposes and relies upon this bodily knowledge.

Although Whitehead does not ever define causal efficacy (it is notable that Whitehead is shy of providing definitions in his philosophy),[1] at one point he describes it as 'our general sense of existence, as one item among others, in an efficacious world' (Whitehead 1978: 178). This 'general sense of existence' comprises a form of knowledge, one that has been ignored by most philosophers. The importance of prepositions is to convey this experience of being one item among others, of being 'with' the world. The body is thus central to Whitehead's philosophical approach. Again, this is not the biological (or 'natural') body; nor is it the phenomenological body (though there are clearly some resonances here). The body (be it animal or human, or

---

1. Except, perhaps, in the splurge of categories that make up the 'Categoreal Scheme' at the start of *Process and Reality* (Whitehead 1978: 20–8).

beyond) is integral to both modes of perception (presentational immediacy and causal efficacy). Indeed, 'the most primitive perception is "feeling the body as functioning." This is a feeling of the world in the past; it is the inheritance of the world as a complex of feeling' (Whitehead 1978: 81). Or, more elegantly: 'We are in the world and the world is in us [. . .] The body is ours, and we are an activity within our body' (Whitehead 1938: 227). The body is a part of the world; it is a portion of the world acting in a specific manner, with specific concerns. Language, as part of the world, is linked to the specificity of the body (as will be discussed in more detail below). Whitehead does not lionise the human body: the 'body is nothing more than the most intimately relevant part of the antecedent settled world' (Whitehead 1978: 64). In order to avoid any bifurcations, it is necessary to widen the scope of the operations and influence of the body, to give it its proper and due place within existence. This involves the development of a prepositional attitude to the body, language and symbolism.

Withness

Despite his development of a full-blown metaphysics (Whitehead 1978), his attempts to rewrite the history and status of science (Whitehead 1932), and his very particular view of the role and status of religion (Whitehead 1927b), Whitehead's writing style is not dogmatic. He does not pronounce the importance of certain ideas, even if they offer radical challenges to usual and accepted modes of thought. This certainly applies in his discussions of the duality of perception. Although this is a key element of his thought that runs throughout both *Symbolism. Its Meaning and Effect* and *Process and Reality*, it often gets overlooked, perhaps as a result of Whitehead's understated style. Whitehead's approach to perception, and the role of the body within this, is, nevertheless, crucial both for his philosophy and for understanding the role and status of both symbolism and language.

Another reason for the overlooking of the duality of perception could be that in our experience, this duality is not to the forefront. This is because our experience becomes unified, becomes *this* experience, through the melding of the two aspects of perception (through what Whitehead calls 'symbolic reference', as will be discussed shortly). Although it is possible to analyse the two modes of perception as separate 'after the event', in most cases our experience is of their interrelation. Thus, Whitehead describes how 'causal efficacy *from* the past is at least one factor giving our presentational immediacy *in* the present. The *how* of our present experience must conform to the *what* of the past in us' (Whitehead 1927a: 58, emphasis in original). Notably, the words that Whitehead highlights are a preposition ('from'), an adverb ('how') and an indication of a substantive ('what'). Experience of the world is a part of the world. It always happens in a certain way (the adverbial); there is both a direction and a connection in experience (the prepositional); such experiences are not fictive or merely subjective, they are utterly real (the substantive). Feelings of the world, by the world, make up the world. This is summed in the title of Whitehead's major work *Process and Reality*.

Whitehead gives a concrete example to explain his more metaphysical point:

> we see *with* our eyes, we taste *with* our palates, we touch *with* our hands, etc.: here the causal efficacy defines regions which are identified with themselves as perceived with greater distinctness by the other mode [presentational immediacy]. To take one example, the slight eye-strain in the act of sight is an instance of regional definition by presentational immediacy. But in itself it is no more to be correlated with projected sight than is a contemporary stomach-ache, or a throb in the foot. The obvious correlation of the eye-strain with sight arises from the perception, in the other mode [causal efficacy], of the *eye* as efficacious in sight. This correlation takes place in virtue of the identity of the two regions, the region of the eye-strain, and the region of the eye-efficacy. (Whitehead 1978: 170, emphasis in original)

'Withness' is, once again, key. Of course, we touch *with* our hands, we see *with* our eyes. The question that Whitehead asks, and to which he responds, is that of *how* we see *with* our eyes. Bodilyness, the activity of the body, is central. However, it plays a dual role through what he refers to as 'eye-strain' and 'eye-efficacy'.

Eye-Strain and Eye-Efficacy

As discussed in Chapter 3, philosophy and science have had problems in accounting for perception, specifically in terms of the 'reality', or otherwise, of the properties or qualities of that which is perceived. For example, is the saltiness of salt located in the atoms that make up the granular substance that is added to food? Or is saltiness some kind of 'psychic addition', an all-too-human contribution to interpreting the world? Can molecules really be said to have a colour? Or is 'greenness' something that humans 'add' to their perception of the world? Whitehead views such questions as arising from incorrect premises; moreover, such questions lead to a bifurcation of human perception from the facticity of the world. Throughout his philosophy, Whitehead seeks to avoid such premises and bifurcations. His discussion of 'eye-strain' is another example of this mode of thinking.

The temptation might be to render Whitehead's notion of presentational immediacy in terms of the human contribution to perception; a quasi-subjective state where the mind entertains, in its own way, immediate displays of colourfulness, taste and so on. Causal efficacy would then be reduced to the enduring world of facticity, shorn from the immediate display of individual human perceptions. This is not the route that Whitehead takes, although he does give some kind of primacy to causal efficacy through the notion of 'bodily efficacy':

> the *'withness' of the body* is an ever-present, though elusive, element in our perceptions of presentational immediacy [. . .]

This component feeling will be called the feeling of bodily efficacy. It is more primitive than the feeling of presentational immediacy which issues from it. Both in common sense and in physiological theory, this bodily efficacy is a component presupposed by presentational immediacy and leading up to it. (Whitehead 1978: 312)

It is the efficacy of the body that is Whitehead's concern, as explained in his example of eye-strain. The primacy of causal or bodily efficacy resides in the enduring experience of having eyes (or hands, or ears, or a tongue, or a nose). We might not always notice that we have such bodily organs; when we are asleep, for example, or even when we are reading a book. However, our ongoing existence relies on and arises from the fact that these hands and eyes 'are mine' (as Descartes puts it). Yet, when reading a book, the light might suddenly change and we need to adjust our eyes; in doing so we would feel some strain within the eye. This feeling of eye-strain is immediate, is contemporary with our perception, and, as such, falls within the realm of presentational immediacy, though it is related to causal efficacy. This is a key point. Whitehead avoids the risks of bifurcation involved in other theories of perception by insisting upon this physical aspect of presentational immediacy, which he describes as 'a physical feeling of a more complex type' (Whitehead 1978: 311). Perception of the contemporary world, in terms of its vivid colour, smells, etc., involves a complex physical feeling. We feel our eyes when seeing, even if only in a negligible manner. This feeling is bodily, but different in kind from the more enduring bodily feeling of causal efficacy. Whitehead makes it clear that his argument is directed against any theory of 'secondary qualities': 'The account given here traces back these secondary qualities to their root in physical prehension expressed by the "*withness* of the body"' (Whitehead 1978: 64).

In *Difference and Repetition*, Deleuze (1994: 211) describes the eye in terms of a solution to the problem of light. Whitehead would not disagree. But he would add that we have a feeling of the eye as both efficacious in sight, and of the region of 'illumination' provided by this instance of eye-strain. We have a feeling of the feeling of the eye; this is the eye-strain. The feeling of the eye-strain is a component in our experience of the immediate colours of the world around us, as presented *by* our eyes, hands and so on. To reiterate:

> The obvious correlation of the eye-strain with sight arises from the perception, in the other mode [causal efficacy], of the *eye* as efficacious in sight. This correlation takes place in virtue of the identity of the two regions, the region of the eye-strain, and the region of the eye-efficacy. (Whitehead 1978: 170, emphasis in original)

There is an inherent duality to perception, as there are two modes of perception, namely, causal efficacy and presentational immediacy, both of which Whitehead describes in terms of prepositions ('with', 'by', 'from'). These prepositions help explain the relationality between the two modes of perception. There is another connection between these modes of perception and 'language', for, as Whitehead puts it: 'The fact the "presentational immediacy" deals with the same datum as does "causal efficacy," gives the ultimate reason why there is a common "ground" for symbolic reference' (Whitehead 1978: 173). This mention of 'symbolic reference' and Whitehead's particular, and generous, account of symbolism will be taken up in the next section.

Symbolism and Symbolic Reference

Whitehead does not doubt the existence or importance of symbolism. Indeed, he sees it as widespread in existence, and this enables him to avoid any charge of bifurcation. Symbolism, signs and communication are not products of human consciousness, human intentions or human interaction. Rather, human consciousness, intentions and interactions are produced by, and within, a more widespread field of symbolism that suffuses existence. Stones, amoeba and trees all engage in some kind of symbolism, although not in such a complex manner as that which is sometimes to be found in human moments of symbolism. By placing symbolism within all existence, Whitehead does not fall prey to the need to explain how humans generate signs, and consequently how these then relate to the things of the world. It is not a question of words or signs capturing, or pointing to, a reality that is 'out there'. Rather, it is a matter of situating human instances of symbolism within a wider framework.

Symbolism is not a placid realm; nothing is, in Whitehead's philosophy. Symbolism constitutes an activity, and this activity is described in terms of 'reference'; hence Whitehead's preferred term to describe the operation of symbolism is 'symbolic reference'. Such reference does not, as is often the case, entail that one thing stands in for another, that a word 'refers' to a thing or a sign to a concept. Whitehead's scheme of symbolism and symbolic reference is much more general. The *reference* of symbolic reference involves the interrelation of the two different modes of perception, as discussed above. This is vital for understanding the role and status of symbolism: 'Symbolic reference between the two perceptive modes affords the main example of the principles which govern all symbolism. The requisites for symbolism are that there be two species of percepta [. . . and that] a correlation between the pair of percepta is established' (Whitehead 1978: 180). Symbolism, in terms of symbolic reference, relies on a very specific form of correlation, one that, as will be seen, does not fall prey to the charge of the correlationist circle as outlined by Meillassoux (2008): 'there is "symbolic reference" between the two species when the perception of a member of one species *evokes* its correlate in the other species' (Whitehead 1978: 181, emphasis added). This is, perhaps, the closest that Whitehead comes to a definition of symbolism; it is the process by which one aspect of experience 'evokes' or 'elicits' another experience. Although not limited to the human level, such an example might illuminate Whitehead's wider point. Hence, he also states: 'The human mind is functioning symbolically when some components of its experience *elicit* consciousness, beliefs, emotions, and usages, respecting other components of its experience' (Whitehead 1927a: 7–8, emphasis added).

To define symbolism in terms of one aspect of experience evoking or eliciting another might, at first sight, appear overly general and lacking in specificity. However, this initial generality works to Whitehead's advantage. Nothing is ruled in or out at this stage. Symbolism is not reliant upon consciousness, subjectivity, culture, meanings or humans. The version of reference that Whitehead develops is radically different from those notions of reference that inform conceptions of signification and also analytic philosophy's attempts to explain the way in which language refers to things. Whitehead's symbolism is not bound to questions regarding representation, correspondence or signification. The democratic approach he sets out does not delimit who or what might be involved in the activity of symbolism; there is no discrimination between pre-existing elements that need to be overcome either through words or signs. Whitehead's point is 'simply' that symbolism and symbolic reference involve one item or element of experience provoking a response beyond the immediacy of that item or experience.

> A flower turns to the light with much greater certainty than does a human being, and a stone conforms to the conditions set by its external environment with much greater certainty than does a flower. A dog anticipates the conformation of the immediate future to his [sic] present activity with the same certainty as a human being. When it comes to calculations and remote inferences, the dog fails. (Whitehead 1927a: 42)

In these examples, Whitehead is discussing his concept of 'conformation', rather than symbolism directly. Nevertheless, this passage comes from his book *Symbolism* and is to be found in a chapter entitled 'Direct Perception of Causal Efficacy' (Whitehead 1927a: 39–43). The comparison of the flower, stone, dog and human acting in relation to causal efficacy gives an indication of Whitehead's understanding of the remit of symbolism throughout existence. Everything, in the sense of every thing, could be said to have the potential to be involved in symbolism, in so far as one element of experience elicits a reaction or response. For the stone, its reaction to the warmth of its environment is minimal. It expands slightly. Flowers follow the sun, more or less accurately, but in different ways, and such a response involves more symbolic reference than in the case of the stone. Dogs would not get excited when their owner picks up the leash if they were not involved in the realm of symbolism. In this case, the leash elicits the positive response from the dog associated with the possibility of a walk. Humans are involved in multiple and complex forms and acts of symbolism, including those of inference and mathematical calculation, as expressed in algebraic symbols, for example.

To avoid any confusion, it is worth making clear that Whitehead's general, yet coherent, account of symbolism does not immediately map on to any more specific theory of signs, or language as a signing system. Perhaps we are so used to thinking of signs and symbols in terms of human communication that any mention of either term elicits questions about what Whitehead would view as a more specific case, namely human versions of symbolism. This does not mean that such accounts are not important. James Williams, for example, in his recent book *A Process Philosophy of Signs* (2016) has developed an open and generous account of signing which could be seen as according with Whitehead's position. For Williams, signs are not limited to, or predicated upon, humans. Signs involve questions of intensity and a Deleuzean diagrammatic. Signs do not have given meanings, but they do come to mean, through the selection of specific elements into a specific set. Williams's account is persuasive but it should be noted that, as he himself makes clear, his philosophical aim is different to that of Whitehead, in that Williams sets out to provide a process account of signs as encountered by humans, rather than a metaphysics within which signs and symbolism have their rightful place. I will return to the distinction between general and local theories of symbolism shortly, after an examination of those moments when Whitehead does discuss words and signs.

Words and Signs

'Considered by themselves the symbol and its meaning do not require *either* that there shall be a symbolic reference between the two, *or* that the symbolic reference between the members of the couple should be one way on rather than the other way on' (Whitehead 1927a: 9–10, emphasis in original). Here, Whitehead is once more operating at a very general level. There is no compulsion or necessity or 'reality' hiding behind the relation between any symbol and its meaning, or any meaning and its symbol. In this way, Whitehead takes the arbitrary character of the sign, as discussed by Saussure, and extends it, even as far as Derrida in his suggestion that human language requires an unspoken and unnoticed 'transcendental signified' (1976: 20) in order to 'shore up the system'. However, Whitehead's metaphysical refiguring of the status of symbolism, and his willingness to allow symbolism to operate throughout existence, without prioritising either human language or consciousness, entails that he has no need of any of the excesses sometimes ascribed to postmodernism. Indeed, Whitehead views himself as an utter 'realist', even if this is a very particular kind of realism; one in which process is reality. Whitehead describes his account of symbolism as 'the foundation of a thorough-going realism. It does away with any mysterious element in our experience which is merely meant, and thereby behind the veil of direct perception' (Whitehead 1927a: 10). His utterly democratic (as opposed to postmodern) approach enables existence to be replete with symbols, and for a vast array of entities to be involved in acts of symbolism. In this way, Whitehead's account of symbolism is distanced from questions about what a sign 'means', or how the mind 'grants meaning to' or 'intends' what it thinks or says. For Whitehead, there is nothing behind the fact that certain instances evoke or elicit novel experiences. This also applies to individual (human) words:

> why do we say that the word 'tree' – spoken or written – is a symbol to us for trees? Both the word itself and trees enter into

our experience on equal terms; and it would be just as sensible, viewing the question abstractedly, for trees to symbolize the word 'tree' as for the word to symbolize the trees. (Whitehead 1927a: 11–12)

It is experience that has priority for Whitehead. Our experience of trees and our experience of the word 'tree' have equal validity within existence. There is no need to prioritise consciousness or the human mind in attempts to locate where the meaning of trees or the word 'tree' resides. Its meaning rests in the experience that is elicited by either the trees or the word 'tree'. In terms of symbolic reference, at the more complex human level, the word 'tree' in a poem may elicit memories of a holiday or when one fell from a tree as a child. Equally, seeing a tree may elicit memories of a poem. 'The word "forest" may suggest memories of forests; but it is just a likely that the sight of a forest, or memories of forests, may suggest the word "forest"' (Whitehead 1978: 182). This mention of forests is germane, as it elicits a text by Kohn (2013) which also attempts to refigure the status of signs, using the work of Peirce rather than that of Whitehead. Kohn asserts in the title of his book that 'forests think', a discussion of which will make up the following section and will allow for an evaluation of Whitehead's contribution to thinking about symbolism.

Do Forests Think?

Kohn's response to this question is resoundingly affirmative, and he uses the work of Peirce to make his case. Peirce was a major philosopher who developed a novel concept of signification, through his development of three distinct but interrelated terms: icon, index, symbol (see, for example, Peirce 1958: 51–4, 391–6). A sustained comparison of the work of Peirce and Whitehead would be a major endeavour and it is not possible to do justice to the intricacies of their similarities and divergences here. Instead, Kohn's reading of Peirce, which itself aims to develop what he calls an 'anthropology beyond the human',[2] will be taken as a way of pointing up some of the resonances between the thought of Peirce and Whitehead.

Like Whitehead, Kohn wants to resituate human language *within* a wider concept of symbolism (or 'semiosis' in Kohn's case). This is not to deny the efficacy of human communication, but to recognise its status as one example of a more general phenomenon. For Whitehead, 'Language is itself a symbolism' (Whitehead 1927a: 61–2). For Kohn:

> representation is something both more general and more widely distributed than human language. It also helps us see that these other modes of representation have properties that are quite different from those exhibited by the symbolic modalities on which language depends [. . .] we need to 'provincialize' language. (Kohn 2013: 38)

Kohn uses the work of Peirce in his attempts to 'provincialize language', as, on Kohn's reading, Peirce, like Whitehead, envisaged 'a special kind of realism that could encompass actual existence within a broader framework that would account for its relationship to spontaneity, growth, and the life of signs in human and nonhuman worlds' (Kohn 2013: 58). Although Whitehead might have some issue with Kohn's use of the term 'representation'[3] and, as will be seen, describing signs as having a 'life' brings its own problems, there are interesting congruences between Kohn's argument and Whitehead's philosophical position. For example, as set out in Chapters 4 and 5, rethinking language involves rethinking both the world and the relation of thought to the world. There is a need to situate thinking within existence. 'Out thoughts are like the world because we are of the world' (Kohn 2013: 60). Or, as Whitehead puts it: 'When it abstracts,

---

2. The subtitle of Kohn's book is 'Toward an Anthropology Beyond the Human'.
3. '"[R]epresentative perception" can never, within its own metaphysical doctrines, produce the title deeds to guarantee the validity of the representation of fact by idea' (Whitehead 1978: 54).

thought is merely conforming to nature – or rather, it is exhibit-
ing itself as an element in nature' (Whitehead 1927a: 25–6). There
is no gulf between thought and the world, as thought is part of
the world (or of 'nature', in the sense of existence). The task at
hand is to establish how such a position relates to language and
words. This is the role of 'signs', according to Kohn and Peirce,
for whom the overarching definition is resolutely pragmatic, in
the philosophical sense of this term: 'A sign has an effect' (Kohn
2013: 33), while Pierce talks of the 'proper significate effect that
the sign produces' (cited in Kohn 2013: 33).

As mentioned previously, Peirce developed a threefold
account of the sign, dividing this wider scheme into icons,
indices and symbols. An icon, for Peirce, 'is in some respect like
its object. That is, it functions as an image when we fail to notice
the difference between it and the event that it represents' (Kohn
2013: 31). Icons do not point to or indicate things in the world.
Instead, they share elements of that which is being signed. This
is a difficult notion but it establishes Peirce's approach as one that
is not premised on a gap between signs and the world, but on a
continuity; something is shared by the sign and what is signed.

The second element of the sign is the index. Kohn gives the
example of a tree branch crashing on to the forest floor. This
was the result of a human cutting a palm tree with the aim of
startling a monkey that was being hunted. 'The crash, as sign,
is not likeness of the object it represents. Instead, it points to
something else. Peirce calls this sort of sign an "Index"' (Kohn
2013: 31). Unlike an icon, which shares some element of the
object that is being signalled, the index opens up possibilities
and points to the future. It calls for interpretations to be made;
and this can be done by humans or monkeys or other creatures;
hence the move beyond an anthropocentric model of the sign.
For the monkey, the crash was a signal (an index of danger) to
which it reacted. There is a clear resemblance here between a sign
eliciting a response and Whitehead's formulation of symbolism
as discussed previously: 'to the extent that indices are noticed
they impel their interpreters to make connections between some

event and another potential one that has not occurred' (Kohn 2013: 32).

The third element of the sign is the symbol:

> Unlike iconic and indexical modes of reference, which form the bases for all representation in the living world, symbolic reference is, on this planet at least, a form of reference that is unique to humans [. . . Symbols] refer to their object indirectly by virtue of the ways in which they relate systematically to other such symbols. Symbols involve conventions. (Kohn 2013: 32)

Notably, in this passage, Kohn uses the same term as Whitehead, namely, 'symbolic reference'. On Kohn's reading, Peircean symbols reside at the more familiar level of human communication and signification. This is not an immediate return to an anthropological model of the sign, for Kohn retains the wider scope of 'semiosis' to describe those occasions on which non-human animals engage in signification. 'Although all life is semiotic, this semiotic quality is amplified and made apparent in the tropical forest, with its unparalleled kinds and quantities of living selves' (Kohn 2013: 78).

Kohn has gained this wider concept of semiosis at a cost. Even if it is allowed that the delimiting of the realm of symbolic reference to humans is valid, the conflation of semiosis with life brings its own problems. It is important not to overstate the case, nor to attempt to completely undermine Kohn and his utilisation of Peirce. The move to dislodge signs and signification from their traditional position as solely creations of human thought and action is laudable and important. In this respect, the appeal to a wider scheme of semiosis is to be welcomed. 'Signs don't come from the mind. Rather, it is the other way around. What we call mind, or self, is a product of semiosis' (Kohn 2013: 34). There is a need to provincialise both language and the mind's relationship to the world. Whitehead would not disagree. But he would urge caution in limiting semiosis to the question of life, for this introduces major difficulties and judgements about that which constitutes life, and what is living, or alive.

Kohn is insistent on such a linking of life and signification: 'Semiosis is the name for this living sign process' (Kohn
2013: 33). His text is peppered with apparently sensible statements regarding the limits of semiosis and the limits of life. For
example: 'Entities that exhibit self-organisation, such as crystals,
snowflakes, or whirlpools, are not alive. Nor, despite their name,
do they involve a self' (Kohn 2013: 55); 'life thinks; stones don't'
(Kohn 2013: 100). Whitehead would not be so dogmatic, or
so sure. This is not to say that Whitehead would vehemently
argue that crystals[4] and whirlpools are alive, or that stones think.
Rather, he would ask what is gained from drawing such sharp
distinctions? At the philosophical level, to conflate semiosis with
life requires a full conceptualisation of what constitutes 'being
alive', which Kohn does not provide. It also introduces sharp
boundaries, or bifurcations, between the animate and the non-
animate that tend to reproduce gulfs or gaps in existence, akin
to the dualisms of the mind/body, nature/social that Whitehead,
and the arguments set out in this book, are at pains to avoid. Such
a boundary is also drawn by Kohn (and perhaps by Peirce) in the
limiting of symbolic reference to humans, which leads Kohn to
assert that a 'dog can understand "sit" without understanding it
symbolically' (Kohn 2013: 53).

As seen in the earlier quotation, Whitehead is prepared to
talk of stones, flowers, dogs and humans within the same ambit.
Of course he recognises that there are major differences in
complexity between the actions and reactions of such entities.
However, given that Whitehead is attempting to develop a
forward-looking metaphysics that avoids the gulfs and bifurcations of modern science and philosophy, he is aware of the
dangers of making somewhat arbitrary, almost *a priori*, categoris-
ations; for example in terms of what is alive or not alive. This
is why Whitehead's extremely general scheme of symbolism,
which might at first sight appear almost tepid, turns out to be

---

4. Whitehead does have interesting things to say about crystals, describing
   them as 'structured societies' (see Whitehead 1978: 99–101).

a bold and radical move that allows for more of existence to be involved in semiosis than is allowed by writers such as Kohn, despite their admirable intention to move 'beyond the human'. Whitehead, in his sometimes understated way, enables us to move well beyond the human.

Conclusion

To claim that Whitehead 'enables us to move well beyond the human' is, perhaps, to go too far too quickly. For it should be recognised that, unlike Kohn and Peirce (or Saussure or James Williams), Whitehead does not attempt to provide a workable model of the operation of signs and symbols within human communication (although he does make some such moves in his chapter 'Uses of Symbolism' (Whitehead 1927a: 60–88)). Accepting Whitehead's general account of symbolism is not enough, of itself, to go beyond the human, in terms of signing and signification. More work needs to be done. However, for the purposes of the arguments set out in this book, what Whitehead highlights is as follows: Within human communication there are myriad symbols. This is not so surprising when it is realised that existence is replete with the symbolic. Symbols are components of the manner, of the adverbial, of 'how' the past proposes itself, and of how we respond to such propositions. Crucially, such responses are not limited to the realm of thought. The body (and not just the human body) is the harbinger of the operations of symbolism. We see, feel, react *with* our bodies. The role of prepositions is to convey this 'withness' in both language and existence.

The next chapter will explore further the status of the body, through an investigation of the role and status of personal pronouns. This will involve rendering elements of Whitehead's work along with elements of feminist critique and philosophy, to investigate, and move beyond, some of the static assumptions lurking behind apparently innocent words such as 'he', 'she' and 'it'.

7

Gender and Personal Pronouns:
She, He, It and They

Personal pronouns appear to indicate who or what acts in the world by standing in for people and things: '*she* kicked the ball', '*he* cooked dinner', '*it* sank', '*they* got married'. Personal pronouns sometimes, but not always, include the 'gender' of the person or object involved. This chapter will analyse what it means to talk of language as 'gendered', and the implications this has for thinking, and living, in the world.

It has become generally accepted within sociology and social theory that it is possible to make a distinction between 'sex' and 'gender'. The term 'sex' refers to the biological or anatomical characteristics of individual humans, usually in terms of their reproductive organs or capacity to procreate. In this sense, 'sex' becomes shorthand for the 'sexual difference' between men and women. This realm is in the purview of science, especially medical science, which seeks to demarcate the biological characteristics of 'man' and 'woman'. Social and cultural scientists, on the other hand, have tended to deal with what they refer to as 'gender'. Anthropologists such as Mead (1949) have described the divergent ways in which different societies or cultures have treated those individuals whom they deem to be 'men' or 'women'. Feminists have used 'sex' and gender to drive a conceptual wedge between the biological and the societal approaches, for example by pointing to the important distinction to be made between two sets of adjectives: 'male' and 'female' and 'masculine' and 'feminine'. These pairs invoke, respectively, the realms of 'sex' and 'gender'. In this argument, it is maintained that variances in attitudes and expectations with regard to gender

110

are not caused by biological factors. If this were the case, there would be no differences between societies and cultures in how they think and act towards men and women, as the same cause would always have the same or similar effect. Also, understandings of what constitutes appropriate gender roles would not have changed over time, if gender were not related to society rather than biology. The task of social and cultural sciences is to map, and perhaps alter, attitudes to what is expected or acceptable in terms of gender and gender roles.

The 'correct' terminology for those individuals who do not fit within the rather static categories of 'man' and 'woman', 'male' and 'female' or 'masculine' and 'feminine' is contested (Whittle 2006) and has recently shifted away from the more medical term 'transsexual' to 'transgender' or 'trans'. Towards the end of this chapter, I will return to such considerations. Before this, it is necessary to investigate the question of gender more closely in terms of a range of questions, such as: What does it mean to talk of gender with regard to language? When we talk of gender in language ('she', 'he') do we mean 'sex' or 'gender'? Is language 'sexed', suggesting that it has some relation to the male or female, or is it 'gendered', suggesting that it is an entirely 'social' affair?

Writing in 1926, in his influential book *A Dictionary of Modern English Usage*, H. W. Fowler provides one answer to such questions, when he states that gender 'is a grammatical term only. To talk of *persons or creatures of the masculine or feminine g[ender]*, meaning *of the male* or *female sex* is either a jocularity (permissible or not according to context) or a blunder' (Fowler 1937: 211). Fowler is drawing on the original Latin meaning of the word *genus* from which the modern word gender is derived. *Genus* indicates a 'type' or 'kind', and is related to the word 'genre'. In this sense, grammatical gender simply indicates a genre, a kind or category into which words are placed. It is entirely social; it refers to the human element of language alone, and the world, once again, does not present itself as it is. Rather, the world is organised according to arbitrary (human) categories, in this case, that of gender, into which different words such as nouns and pronouns are sifted and sorted. To ask if such genders, genres or categories are, of themselves, biologically 'sexed' is, for Fowler, a mistake, even a joke. In those languages which refer to the sun in 'masculine' terms and the moon in the 'feminine', it is not that these two objects are in themselves male or female. It is simply a matter of a human placement of differing categories upon a world that is resolutely unconcerned and uninvolved in such classifications. To believe that language is gendered, in the sense of being 'sexed', is to misunderstand the status of grammar.

Fowler's suggestion would seem to be that other words could have been adopted for these classifications. Perhaps nouns might be categorised in terms of 'up', 'down' and 'middle', instead of 'masculine', 'feminine' and 'neuter'. The sun might be of the 'up' gender, the moon of the 'down' gender, while those items currently described as neuter would be ascribed to the 'middle' gender. This raises the question of why the specific terms 'masculine', 'feminine' and 'neuter' were chosen to divide up language and the world. There is the secondary question, of whether even if 'up', 'down' and 'middle' had been selected, would there not be some kind of hierarchy between these (where 'up' is taken to be better than 'down')? These words have meanings and connotations that carve up both language and the world in a very particular way.

Rethinking 'Sex' and Gender

Although many sociologists ascribe the establishment of the distinction between 'sex' and gender to Simone de Beauvoir in her 1949 text *The Second Sex*, this division is not as clear-cut in de Beauvoir's work as is sometimes thought to be the case. This is not to suggest that making a distinction between 'sex' and gender is wrong, but it does need to be approached with care.

In the Introduction to the first volume of *The Second Sex*, de Beauvoir states that her main aim is to ask (and respond to) the question: 'What is a woman?' (de Beauvoir 1988: 13). In the

Introduction to the second volume, she writes: 'When I use the words *woman* or *feminine* I obviously refer to no archetype, no changeless essence' (de Beauvoir 1988: 31, emphasis in original). De Beauvoir argues that the question of the existence, and the experience of the existence, of 'woman' has not previously been addressed. There is a lack of thought about *both* the status of 'woman' and the lives of women. However, de Beauvoir does not make a strict division between these two elements. She does not reduce the question of what a woman 'is' to the biological ('sex'); likewise, the lived societal experience of women ('gender') is not purely social. To immediately separate off the anatomical from the societal or cultural leads to the creation of two worlds: the natural and the social. 'Sex', in the sense of sexual difference, would fall under the remit of biology, of the natural. Gender would be located in the realm of the social, to be studied by sociology and cultural studies. This produces another bifurcation, a powerful and insidious one. In this instance the sexed body is placed in the real world, while gender only exists in the words and language deployed to conceptualise, and to talk of, this other world. Once again, words and things have been divided; on this occasion the gulf pivots around questions of biological sexual difference and gender.

This is not the position that de Beauvoir develops, even though traces of this apparently straightforward split resonate throughout many subsequent sociological readings of 'sex' and gender. De Beauvoir's stance provides a more complex account in which it is not always clear where the body ends and society begins. De Beauvoir is, however, very precise in her melding, and this leads her to an important perspective on the interrelations of language and the world, of words and things.

> A man would never set out to write a book on the peculiar situation of the human male. But if I wish to define myself, I must first of all say: 'I am a woman' [. . .] A man never begins by presenting himself as an individual of a certain sex; it goes without saying that he is a man. The terms *masculine* and *feminine* are used symmetrically only as a matter of form, as on legal

113

papers. In actuality the relation of the two sexes is not quite like that of two electrical poles, for man represents both the positive and the neutral [. . .] whereas woman represents only the negative. (de Beauvoir 1988: 15, emphasis in original)

Men take their status as both humans and as men for granted. For example, men do not have to explain that they are writing 'as a man'. It is seen as normal, as 'natural' even. The fact that the writer is male has no bearing on what he is writing, so it is not even worth mentioning. Women do not share this privilege; they are immediately seen as 'women writers'. Their thoughts and writings do not come out of nowhere (as appears to be the case for men); they are not pure and objective (as male writers might claim for themselves); they always come from somewhere. This somewhere is tied up, somehow, with them being women, which, in turn, appears to refer to the biological. They are *women* writers.

De Beauvoir's analysis invokes the terms 'masculine' and 'feminine', and, as has been seen, these have often been taken to refer to the gendered element of the argument. This involves a description of a particular kind of society, one in which such terms are used in legal documents, for example. Yet masculine and feminine are not opposites with equal weight, as is the case with the plus and minus associated with positive and negative electrical charges. De Beauvoir is relying upon a factor in the French language which is not, at first sight, as evident in English. It also links to the subject matter of this chapter, as set out in its title, namely, personal pronouns.

The French for 'he' is *il*. Yet the same term is used even when the gender of the thing or person in question is not known. All nouns are gendered in French and, in the case of a dog, the noun is masculine (*le chien*). There is also a French word for a 'female' dog, namely, *la chienne*. However, this word would only be used if the speaker had the extra knowledge that the dog were female; it is not something that is assumed. When asking if someone has a dog, the masculine form would be used, as this is assumed to be the normal situation. The female dog is an exception.

De Beauvoir's point is reinforced by the fact that this also applies when there is no apparent noun (or subject); for example, when commenting on an apparently neutral state of affairs such as 'it is warm' or 'it is raining'. In both cases, the masculine form *il* would be used to stand it for 'it' (*il fait chaud, il pluie*). The masculine element incorporates both those things that are known to be male (men and dogs) and also those situations where the gender is not known, or is deemed irrelevant. There is an imbalance between the masculine and the feminine; they are not reflections of each other. Worse, the masculine becomes the default position, the norm, while the feminine is only used to indicate those peculiar, uncommon occurrences where women, the female or the feminine are involved. It is this peculiarity that, according to de Beauvoir, makes it possible to describe the feminine as representing the unusual, the exception, as that which deviates from the norm. De Beauvoir suggests that this entails that the female and the feminine is regarded as an aberration.

This difficulty is particularly acute when it comes to the personal pronoun word 'they' (the third person plural). In French, if all members of the group are male the word *ils* is used; if they are all female, then *elles* is used. A problem arises when the group is mixed. There is no word in French that indicates the mix of the masculine and feminine or men and women, in a group; instead, the long-standing rule is to deploy the masculine plural, *ils*. The feminine is subsumed into the masculine. This imbalance is not just evident in French but in a range of European languages, and probably beyond. Furthermore, in many languages (especially certain Slavic ones) it applies not only to 'he', 'she', 'they' and 'it' but to possessive pronouns and verbs. The Czech writer Jindra Tichý has pointed out the absurdity of the situation with regard to verbs through the consideration of two apparently very similar sentences:[1]

---

1. Tichý's article is available at http://nb.vse.cz/kfil/elogos/logpoint/94-3/ NTICHA.htm (accessed 22 July 2019).

All the women of the world went for a walk.

In Czech this would read:

Všechny ženy světa šly na proházku.

Tichý presents a second sentence:

John and all the women of the world went for a walk.

In Czech this would read:

John a všechny ženy světa šli na proházku.

The difference lies in the change of the past tense of the verb 'to go' (*jít*).[2] In the situation involving 'only' all the women of the world, the feminine form of the verb in the plural is used (*šly*). However, when *one* man tags along with all the women of the world, the verb has to change to reflect the presence of this one man, and so the masculine form of the verb is used (*šli*). Tichý points out that it only takes one man to be present for the activity of all the women of the world to be incorporated into the masculine form.

These examples demonstrate how widespread and influential are the problems of gender in terms of 'sex', in both language and the world, remembering that language is part of the world. Problems with inequality in language are also problems in the world. These discrepancies lurk in our thought, language and lives. As the francophone Belgian philosopher Luce Irigaray puts it:

> we argue and debate within a field and with logical and grammatical tools defined in such a way that we cannot really think. The horizon of understanding we have debars us from that thought. We discuss, we reason, but we do not think. (Irigaray 1996: 36)

---

2. The verb 'to go' (*jít*) is irregular in Czech, hence the different form of the past participle, namely, *šel*.

116

Grammar, logic and the world hinder us in our thinking. For Irigaray, grammar is based on a difference between the sexes that is unrealistic, as it does not see male and female (or masculine and feminine) as either equals or as different and yet, if not equal, then at least having their own integrity. Grammar does not grant a positive content to both of the terms 'masculine' and 'feminine'. Instead, the latter is viewed as an insipid reflection of the former and can be subsumed into it. Our grammar priori- tises the male and sometimes hides behind a supposedly neutral (or neuter) term to disguise this. This has consequences not just for our words, thought and language but for the world.

Like de Beauvoir, Irigaray argues that the concept of 'woman' and the lived experience of women have not been given suf- ficient conceptual exploration or status in the world. Irigaray is explicit in her refusal of any simple division between 'sex' and gender when addressing such concerns.

> Given the way that our society is structured – men were, when young, totally dependent on women. They use them for succour and support to become what they are. Then leave them out of public life. This is more than just gender. This is how the world is (ontologically). (Irigaray 1993: 78)

As Whitford (1991) makes clear, when reading (or translating) both de Beauvoir and Irigaray, attention needs to be paid to the specific meanings of the words that they use; for example *sexe, féminin, genre*.[3] These might seem to map on to the English words 'sex', 'feminine' and 'gender'. But they do not. *Sexe* can refer to genitals, but it also has a wider scope and can overlap with some elements of the English term 'gender'. *Féminin* can be translated as either feminine or female, and it is not always clear, except from context, whether reference is being made to the supposedly 'natural' or 'societal' element. *Genre* does not im- mediately or only mean 'gender'. It encompasses the original

---

3. Margaret Whitford has provided a very helpful glossary of these and other terms in her collection of essays by Irigaray (see Whitford 1991).

Latin sense of 'type' or 'kind', as discussed earlier. Importantly, in French, *genre* can also refer to grammatical gender. Such intricacies are important when considering the abiding problem of whether language is 'sexed' or gendered and how this relates to the real people of the world. This has been an enduring concern of Irigaray for over forty years, from a rereading of the philosophical, scientific and psychoanalytic canon of Western thought to contemporary politics (Irigaray 1985a; 1985b; 1993; 1994; 1996; 2000a; 2000b).

Job Titles

With regard to language and the world, lives and grammar, Irigaray gives the example of how, in both French and English syntax, an occupation is often regarded as a kind of possession (as discussed in the previous chapter, Dewey would also question the metaphysical accuracy of such an approach). Grammatically speaking, it can seem as if the subject (the 'I') possesses an object (the occupation) – 'I *have* a job as a baker.' Irigaray argues that maleness is, surreptitiously perhaps, expressed in this situation. Not only, practically and historically speaking, have most occupations tended to be held by men (butchers, bakers and candlestick-makers) but, as with de Beauvoir, the normal and the neutral have been regarded as male. The female is only remarked upon as accidental or unusual. This is more evident in French where the person who has the occupation is usually referred to as male, while the field or area in which a person works (the occupation itself) is taken to be female. The default noun for a doctor (*le médecin*) takes the masculine form while the realm of medicine (*la médicine*) takes the feminine (Irigaray 1993: 128). Irigaray points to other, almost paradoxical, situations. For example, in French it is possible to hold the occupation of café-owner (*un cafetier*). However, to be a specifically female café-owner would be to be *une cafetière*, which, in both English and French, means coffee-pot. The specifically female café-owner is an impossibility, as the word is already taken by a different 'feminine' object – a coffee-pot (Irigaray 1994: 50), something which can be possessed but cannot be lived. Irigaray thinks that this is a serious problem not only because it means that language is unbalanced but because this instantiates a genuine imbalance in the world.

At this stage of the discussion, however, the objection might be raised that Irigaray's (and perhaps de Beauvoir's) analysis might have some force when analysing Francophone societies, but it has limited relevance to the Anglophone world. There are two possible responses to such claims. The second, which will be dealt with below, involves Irigaray's arguments regarding the status of 'sexed' human subjects ('man' and 'woman'). A first response can be found in a consideration of personal pronouns.

Gendered English

The use of personal pronouns, such as 'he', 'she', 'it' and 'they', in English, has changed over time. For example, in the previous chapter, quotations were offered from John Dewey that included the following phrases: 'houses are usually owned, are mine and yours and *his*'. The assumption seems to be that women do not own houses. Elsewhere Dewey writes: 'Nature is kind and hateful, bland and morose, irritating and comforting, long before *she* is mathematically qualified.' These are occasions when gender is used in English. Nature is female, it is claimed, because 'she' is to do with reproduction, regeneration. This is compounded by the related idea that such nature is studied by *'men* of science', as Whitehead unfortunately puts it (Whitehead 1964: 29). Of course, Dewey and Whitehead were writing in a different era. Things have changed. A danger, however, lies in assuming that there is some smooth trajectory towards equality that somehow plays out through the unfolding of reason, so that various societies become more aware of the reasonableness of countering gender inequality in the world and in the way that we talk about the world. Nevertheless, the very fact that the use of personal pronouns has changed demonstrates that their meaning and usage is not fixed; it is something that can be contested. Such contestations have a history which is, in itself, informative.

Returning to H. W. Fowler, in his *Dictionary of Modern English Usage*, he states:

> Everyone knows the inconvenience of being uncertain whether a doctor is a man or a woman; hesitation in establishing the word *doctress* is amazing. Far from needing to reduce the number of our sex-words, we should do well to indulge in real neologisms such as *teacheress, singeress* and *danceress*. (Fowler, cited in Marsh 2014: 232)

The multiplying of terms for women performing certain occupations or roles might appear quaint, if not ridiculous. Writing 'as a man', as de Beauvoir might put it, Fowler's initial concern, presumably, is that he might be embarrassed when having to be treated by a medical doctor who happens to be a woman. Yet it may well be the case that certain people, on certain occasions, would prefer to see a doctor of the same 'sex' or gender. I will consider this point in more detail after a brief detour through the world of actors and actresses.

David Marsh, while in the role of production editor of *The Guardian* newspaper, insisted that journalists should never use the word 'actress' but only that of 'actor'.[4] One reason for this is that the word 'actress' is seen as limiting. In a theatre company, to describe a person as the best actress is to compare them to the other female actors in the group. To call someone the best actor

---

4. Marsh uses the rather 'local' example of the British cast of the series of *Carry On* films to make his point. 'If I describe Hattie Jacques as the finest actress in the *Carry On* films, I am judging her against the likes of Joan Sims, Barbara Windsor and (the criminally underrated) Patsy Rowlands. If I declare her to be the finest *Carry On* actor, I am saying Hattie's body of work was not just better than the other women's, but superior to those of Kenneth Williams, Sidney James and Charles Hawtrey as well' (Marsh 2014: 231).

is not simply to state that they are the best male actor, but that they are the best at acting in the company. The female has been subsumed into the male, in a manner akin to that described by de Beauvoir and Irigaray. The masculine term (actor) can include the female, but not the other way around. If both words are in current usage, then there is an asymmetry between 'actor' and 'actress'. Actor also stands in for the neuter (where the gender of the person acting is not known), so the balance is skewed. Given that those individuals working in the theatre and cinema are performing comparable roles, the argument is that they should all be called 'actors' (and paid equally for equal work).

This seems like a cogent argument, and it echoes the thoughts of de Beauvoir on the asymmetry inherent in language and the world. However, it is important to be aware of its limitations and consequences. The specific history of our society and our language is one in which most occupations, such as that of doctor, teacher and actor, were carried out by men. Women, and the female version, were rare, even peculiar. They needed further explanation (hence Fowler's demand for 'doctresses'). Apparently neutral words, such as actor, provide a yardstick that may not immediately appear to refer to the male, or to be masculine; but in so far as women are not immediately seen as fully representative of the weight of these words, then language is indeed sexed or gendered since it tends to favour the male or masculine aspect. Insisting immediately upon a general imposition of one singular term may pay lip-service to the problem of language and gender, but may also ignore the more fundamental problem.

This leads Irigaray to suggest that there is a need to develop and express specific female (or feminine) subject positions. Paradoxically (for some), this means that she outlines a position that is not so dissimilar from that of Fowler when he advocated the proliferation of titles for female holders of certain occupations. The concern, for Irigaray, is that recognition of the specific contribution or approach of women in and to the world is in danger of being reduced or subsumed by their being incorporated within a male (or masculine) term. To avoid this, the female aspect needs to be given its due, with its own words and terms, and not swept under the masculine conceptual carpet. The spirit in which Irigaray makes her argument is radically different from that of Fowler. 'I suggest that the following law be passed: The mixed plural will be masculine [*ils*] one year; feminine [*elles*] the next' (Irigaray 1994: 49). It is important, however, to recognise that this would only constitute one very small step. To think that the problems lie in language alone, and that, if language were correctly policed, the inequalities of the world would somehow disappear, is to be disingenuous at best. According to Irigaray, the task is to change the world-as-it-is-now so that it is possible to become full human subjects.

> Sexual difference cannot [. . .] be reduced to a simple extra-linguistic fact of nature. It conditions language and is conditioned by it. It not only determines the system of pronouns, possessive adjectives, but also the gender of words [. . .] It's situated at the junction of nature and culture. (Irigaray 1993: 20)

Sexual difference is not a fact of nature, separate from language. Sexual difference does not simply determine language, but nor is language separate from the actuality of sexual difference. Irigaray is pointing towards the complexity of the interrelations of language and the world, of words and things. As Irigaray makes clear, our real bodies and our actual words come together to make the world-as-it-is-now. This is not dissimilar from the ideas of Whitehead, Deleuze and Dewey, as discussed in previous chapters. The added layer is that some of these 'things' are what we think of, and speak of, as human subjects.

Some have taken issue with Irigaray and her insistence that the primary fact of sexual difference is the difference between men and women, or between man and woman; for example when she writes: 'a double nature exists, a masculine and a feminine nature' (Irigaray 2000a: 47). Irigaray places great emphasis on the need to develop relations between these two: 'We are all of us, men and women alike, sexed. Our principal task is to make the transition from nature to culture as sexed beings, to become women and men while remaining faithful to our gender' (Irigaray 1996: 30). For many commentators, this means that Irigaray not only assumes that the most fundamental couple is a heterosexual one, thereby relegating homosexual relations to a secondary position, but she completely overlooks the status of intersexed and transgender individuals. Such criticisms certainly have some weight and it is not my intention to completely defend Irigaray. The reliance upon the relations between 'man and woman' as foundational is troublesome.

At the same time, Irigaray's work helps to develop a way of taking the relations between language, bodies and the world seriously. Language and our bodies are not separate as 'language [. . .] is made flesh in you, in me, in us' (Irigaray 2000b: 19). Moreover, Irigaray clarifies that altering language alone is not enough; it is always a matter of language and the world, and the complex relations between the two. For the arguments being set out in this book, Irigaray's importance lies in her utter refusal of the bifurcation of either 'sex' and 'gender' or nature and culture. In this way, she follows and extends Whitehead's protest against the implicit and unwarranted fault-line of modern thought which separates, or bifurcates, the real from experiences of the real, things from their properties, the world from language. Avoiding such separations is no easy task, and Irigaray's alternative might not be wholly successful. Yet she is resolute in facing up to the difficulties involved in such a project. One example of this is the insistence that matters of 'sex', 'gender' and language do not lie in the realm of either nature or culture. What is required is a rethinking of this apparent dichotomy. Irigaray does not want to erase or deconstruct the concepts of man and woman but to rethink them, retaining elements of what is supposedly captured by the terms 'sex' and 'gender'. She attempts this by deploying the term 'sexuate': 'I am sexuate, I am not neuter, anonymous or interchangeable' (Irigaray 2000b: 39). And: 'I am asking to be recognized as really an other, irreducible to the masculine subject' (Irigaray 2000a: 124). Her protest, as discussed

123

previously, is against the subsumption of the female aspect into the male or masculine, for example through the unthinking use of neutral terms which, in fact, are biased towards the male. To achieve this, Irigaray sets out to develop a model of female subjectivity that is different from, and not reducible to, the model of subjectivity that has, until now, been taken as universal, when it is, she argues, only partial, only masculine.

Irigaray maintains that predominant conceptions of what it means to be a (human) subject, an 'I', have been characterised, both in thought and speech, on a model of the male (or *masculin*). This has involved treating women and the word 'woman' as secondary. Irigaray's tracing of the wide-ranging, but often unnoticed, ways in which subjectivity has been characterised as male or masculine is sustained, powerful and complex, and it is not possible to do justice to it here (for a fuller reading, see Halewood 2011a: 125–46; Stone 2006; Whitford 1991). The previous chapter outlined Whitehead's insistence on the centrality of the 'withness' of the body, both to existence and thought. Irigaray characterises the traditional model of Western philosophy and science in similar terms, for example, in the lack and denigration of the role of the body as is to be found in Plato:

> *Blind* except for the contemplation of his Ideas. *Deaf* except to the sounds of his soul revolving in harmony, and the soul speaks only to itself without the aid or assistance of any voice. Thought now capable of doing without 'discourse' or 'dialogue' [. . .] *Without hands or feet*, organs, unfitted to the movements of intelligence and reflection [. . .] *Taking care not to touch* any 'strange things,' also, and *deprived of legs* so that there can be no walking off toward something attractive outside the self. Completeness of one who is self-sufficient: this is the destiny to which the souls are called who have donned the nature of the living beings most able to honor the Gods. (Irigaray 1985a: 321, emphasis in original)

The masculine bias of philosophy is expressed in a 'withoutness' of the body. The task, which resonates with Whitehead's approach, is to develop a philosophy that can incorporate the 'withness' of the body and deal with the implications of recognising bodilyness as a crucial and enduring factor in existence and our lives.

A crucial and distinct element of Irigaray's thought is the appeal to develop ways of thinking and speaking that start from the position of women and woman. What is (again) controversial in Irigaray's argument is that, in order to do this, it is necessary to start from the status of women's bodies. Western thought and language have started from a supposition of that which constitutes the male body: 'the fundamental model of the human being [. . .] one, singular, solitary and historically masculine, that of the adult Western male, rational and competent' (Irigaray 2000a: 122). The male (or masculine) subject has been taken as singular and complete. Irigaray argues that, in order to challenge this, it is necessary for women to start thinking, talking and acting in a way that avoids this singularity, as epitomised by the male body. The starting point that she advocates is the specific status of women's bodies. The advantage of this is summed up in the title of one of Irigaray's most important books – *This Sex Which Is Not One*. Irigaray believes that women's bodies are not reducible or explainable in terms of the unity that men claim for themselves or for their language. Men have one penis. Women's sex organs are not unitary: 'She has at least two of them, but they are not identifiable as ones. Indeed she has many more. Her sexuality, always at least double, goes even further, it is *plural*' (Irigaray 1985b: 28, emphasis in original).

The problem, for some feminists, is that this seems to put us back into the realm of the 'natural' body. This runs the risk of returning to a position where men and women have radically different biological make-ups, which lead them to think and behave in different ways (men are built to be hunters, to be aggressive: women are built to bear children, to be caring). This is exactly what the distinction between sex and gender was meant to help overcome. However, Irigaray thinks that this distinction can itself be problematic and limiting.

The difficulties women have in gaining recognition for their social and political rights are rooted in this insufficiently thought out relation between biology and culture. At present, to deny all explanations of a biological kind – because biology has para-doxically been used to exploit women – is to deny the key to interpreting this exploitation. (Irigaray 1993: 46)

Taken in the light of Whitehead's critique of the bifurcation of nature, this can be read in a way that does not resort to bio-logical essentialism but, rather, recognises that an easy separation of nature from culture is an expression of a deeper problem, one that is to do with some of the complexities of thinking about the relation of language and the world, as set out in previous chapters.

Irigaray focuses on one specific iteration of these relations, namely whether the things of the world, including human subjects, are sexed or gendered, and how language is implicated in this, or even limits thought. The importance of Irigaray lies in the insistence that any attempt to simply erase or efface current inequalities between men and women, or between the genders, by adopting supposedly neutral terms, is to misunderstand the problem. Tinkering with language to avoid or remove words or phrases that are considered inappropriate or offensive is not enough. What is required is a change in thinking, speaking and being; this will involve changing the world.

Telling Others What to Say, and Think

The question of whether it is worthwhile or valid to remark upon and criticise how others speak is a contentious issue. For some, grammar is purely descriptive; the task for linguistics is only to outline the syntax and semantics that people use. If those living in twenty-first-century Britain choose to use the word 'literally' to mean 'figuratively', then so be it. On the other hand, there are those who believe that grammar, syntax and semantics form an ordered system with its own logic and rules.

These need to be regulated and reinforced, with 'errors' being corrected. This is the prescriptive approach. It is important to note, however, that discussions that are often held to be about grammar are not actually to do with the grammatical structure of a language. For example, the changing meaning of a word, such as 'literally', is concerned with semantics rather than grammatical structure. Strictly speaking, grammarians would limit themselves to instances such as the assertion that it is forbidden to ever split an infinitive, or to split an infinitive, ever. Most 'liberal-minded' writers tend towards seeing grammar as descriptive and believe prescriptive grammarians to be outdated and doomed in their misguided attempts to apply the rules and rigours that often derive from a dead language, Latin, to the living, breathing phenomenon that is English today.

One current example is the personal pronoun 'they', with its related possessive pronoun 'their'. It is generally accepted that it is a mistake to use a plural to refer to a singular. However, when it comes to describing an individual whose 'sex' or 'gender' is not known, this raises a problem. On hearing unexpected footsteps in one's house, a person might comment – 'There is someone coming up the stairs.' But what if I am worried that the person is a burglar? Should I say – 'I wonder if they [the 'someone'] have come to rob us?' This is technically incorrect, according to some grammarians; the plural 'they' has been used when only one set of footsteps was heard, and the individual pronoun, 'someone', has been used previously. As a result, the singular, either 'he' or 'she', should have been used. Would it be better to say 'I wonder if he has come to rob us?' or 'I wonder if she has come to rob us?' It may well be that most burglars in the UK are male, but does that warrant jumping to a linguistic conclusion? Most burglars are under 35. Would this justify saying 'I wonder if that male under 35 has come to rob us?' This may seem like an abstruse example, but the reach of the question is more widespread than might first be thought.

The dichotomy between 'he' and 'she' does not reflect the range of possible experiences of people in the world. Writers such as Whittle (2006) point out that personal pronouns are limiting and exclusionary for some of those who identify as 'trans' and who do not want to be reduced, necessarily, either to 'he' or 'she', sometimes preferring the word 'they' or neologisms (such as 'per') to be used as the relevant pronoun. What is noticeable in such arguments is that this involves a prescriptive approach to grammar; it requires 'telling' people what words to use, or not use. Yet the prescriptive approach, that of enforcing rules, has long been associated with a conservative view that looks backward to a logic in the English language that needs to be preserved. In the case of the personal pronoun 'they', such concerns can be partially assuaged by the examples from Lewis Carroll, Shakespeare, the Authorised Version of the Bible and Thackeray that Marsh (2014: 229–30) cites, to demonstrate that the practice of using this term to refer to individuals has a long history.

Nevertheless, the idea that language should be 'policed' is not wedded to either a conservative or a more liberal viewpoint. As has been seen, Irigaray, and other feminists such as Spender (1980), insist that language needs to be altered, as does the world. Resistance to such prescriptive changes can come from those who argue *against* what has been called 'political correctness', citing instances such as the 'banning' of the word 'chairman' to refer to the person who runs a committee, irrespective of their 'sex' or gender. This is an instructive example. In most universities in the UK, it is common to call the person who is taking a meeting the 'chair', rather than 'chairman' or 'chairwoman'. The chair has the responsibility and the right to set the agenda, guide discussion, and to help inform decisions. The chair has a certain authority. This raises the question of what kind of authority is held by the chair. As is often the case, the history of the word, and the worlds in which that word have operated, are informative.

The word 'chair' is ultimately derived from the Latin term *cathedra*, as in the related English word 'cathedral'. Indeed, there is an overlap between the two terms. A cathedral marks the place where the power and authority of a bishop resides; it also indicates the area over which the bishop can exercise their authority, their diocese. A diocese can also be referred to as a 'see', which itself is derived from the Latin for seat (*sedes*). Chairs and seats are tied up with the authority of the Christian Church. In fact, there really are (or were) chairs in cathedrals from which bishops speak. The actual chair from which pronouncements are made encapsulates the authority of the Church, enabling what is said to hold weight, truth and power. Moreover, this kind of authority has been resolutely male, for at least two reasons. First, all bishops (until recently) have been men. Second, the kind of authority exercised by the Christian Church represents a model of power, located in a central authority (the chair), which is associated with how masculinity has been understood in the West. Bishops represent a kind of masculine authority and the authority of a bishop's chair reinforces a specific kind of masculinity.

This is not only of theological interest. Professors at universities are still called 'chairs' in their official titles. Stephen Hawking held the Lucasian Chair in Mathematics at the University of Cambridge, which was founded in 1663 by Henry Lucas. This chair was also held by Isaac Newton. It is not an overstatement to assert that it is the chair that makes someone a professor. As was the case with bishops, there used to be actual chairs in which professors sat, although this is rarely the situation today. Such chairs grant an authority that is analogous to that of a bishop. Indeed, this is its derivation, in that Western universities were originally institutions within the Christian Church, designed to further theological knowledge and train *men* for their roles in the Church. The cloisters and quadrangles at older universities such as Oxford and Cambridge, with their similarities to monastery buildings, are reminders of this. Nowadays, the domain (or diocese) within which a professor has authority is often still made explicit in their full title: Professor of Ancient History, Professor of Modern Social Theory, etc. The form of professorial authority still bears the traces of its origin and enables a professor to profess, to state their own ideas with authority; an authority that is ultimately derived from their chair. In one important sense, the authority held by professors is male *and* masculine. It is derived from that of bishops; most professors have been (and still are) men; the kind of authority incorporated in a professorship models a traditional view of masculinity (professors do not like being contradicted).

This is why questions as to whether to say 'chairman', 'chair-woman' or simply 'chair' are not only to do with language. They are tied up with our history, our world as it was and as it is now. As a result, it might well be better to talk of actors and chairs rather than to invent female versions of these words. However, this is not the whole answer, for, as we have seen, the words and things (the people and their chairs) are implicated within a form of authority that is closely tied to our understandings of what it means to be a man and a woman. It is necessary to recognise the specificity of the model of (masculine) authority implicated in the chairs of bishops, professors and committees. This mention of specificity is important. As Donna Haraway, in a slightly different context, puts it: 'all dreams for a perfectly true language, of perfectly naming experience [. . .] are totalizing and imperialist' (1991: 173). To treat language as a system, dislocated from the world, or from worlds with their particular histories, and to claim that language can be cleansed or purified, separately from its specific legacies, would be both to bifurcate language from the world and attempt to impose abstract answers on to concrete problems.[5] Each instance needs to be dealt with on its own merits, and language is not to be separated from the world that enables it to express and be expressed.

---

5. As has been argued throughout this chapter, even within the English language the question of gender is involved more often than might be first thought. For example, when I originally wrote the previous sentence, I used the phrase 'is to be naïve at best'. Perhaps because my mind is focused on issues of grammar and gender, I became uneasy about the word 'naïve' and checked its origin. It comes from the French *naif*. This is the masculine version, but in English the feminine form 'naïve' has been adopted. Although not immediately obvious, to be naïve is, in some way, linked with the feminine. This is reinforced by the retention, in English, of

Conclusion

Building on ideas developed throughout this book, this chapter has argued that questions and problems involving words and things take on a new slant when the matter of concern becomes human individuals and how to refer to them, through personal pronouns for example. It has been argued that avoiding gendered constructions might appear to reduce the 'gender problem' in English, but that is actually to remain at the level of language alone. The things of the world have dropped out of the picture. In this case, these things are actual, individual humans – men, women and those who identify as neither. Reducing references to gender is not necessarily an advantage; it might suggest an erasure of women from the scene of writing and speaking, by making this scene entirely neuter, and therefore, following de Beauvoir and Irigaray, resolutely male. To put it bluntly, and invoking another set of ideas, it is certainly possible for politicians, police officers or journalists to learn to talk about 'ethnic communities' rather than about 'coloureds', 'Asians' or worse. But this does not mean that the way they think and act in the world has changed.

Returning to the question of 'sex' and 'gender', the extent to which these are concepts or 'things' that permeate the world and language is still unclear. The work of Irigaray is useful in pointing to the complex relations between language and different forms of subjectivity. However, Irigaray's analysis relies on the difference between 'masculine' and 'feminine' as being foundational, and this aspect needs reorienting. Remaining faithful to the idea that language is an element of the world and that the world is not fixed makes it possible to consider how human bodies come to be. This does not necessarily entail starting with the notions of

---

the masculine version 'naif', even if it is rarely used. When searching for an alternative word, I considered 'disingenuous', which is equally problematic in that it is again derived from a feminine form of a French word – *ingénue*. In both English and French this refers to an inexperienced girl or young woman.

'man' and 'woman'. Rather, man and woman are outcomes, and they are not the only possible outcomes. The processes that go into creating such outcomes involve both language and material bodies. We become actual men, women, trans, indeed more or otherwise, on different occasions and in different ways. The role of the adverbial comes to the fore once again. The processes involved are neither 'natural' nor 'social'. Language and the world become together; in doing so, they express those elements that later come to be called natural and social. The perspective needs to be shifted. The natural and social, 'sex' and gender, are not generative but are themselves things that come to be. Man and woman are not ideas or entities that exist continually. They come to be at different points and different times. This is something that Irigaray acknowledges in part, though only within the limits of a firm distinction between man and woman. For example: 'each man must remain a man in the process of becoming. He himself has to accomplish the task of being *this* man he is by birth and a model of humanity, a model that is both corporeal and spiritual' (Irigaray 1996: 27, emphasis in original). Such processes are, according to Irigaray, more 'straightforward' than those involving woman: 'puberty, loss of virginity, maternity, menopause, – stages requiring a more complex becoming than that of man' (Irigaray 2000a: 131).

It would, however, be necessary to extend Irigaray's analysis so that other ways of coming-to-be were recognised and made possible. Other kinds of bodies can become; transgendered and intersexed, for example. This would also apply to questions of sexuality, so that an individual's sexuality is no longer envisaged as fixed. It is not a question of whether sexual inclinations are innate or culturally acquired. Such an approach would again be to indulge in a primary bifurcation. We become straight, gay, lesbian or otherwise over and over again, at different points and in different ways. This is an important point that has implications for debates between some feminists and some trans activists over whether someone who identifies as a different gender to that which was ascribed to them at birth is, for example, a 'real' woman. The reading of Whitehead offered throughout this book would suggest that there is a need to shift the way in which such debates are set up. It might be better to move beyond any assumption of the fixity of the concept of man or woman to a recognition of the complex processes that go into, or limit, how individual humans become male, female, trans or otherwise. This is not argue that it is possible to smooth out inequalities simply by stating that 'it is all a question of process'. To adopt a processual view is not to indulge in the worst excesses of either postmodernism or cultural relativism. What is required is an understanding of the specific and different manners of processes that have been possible, are currently possible, and that could be made possible.

A second important point that can be taken from Whitehead (and Haraway 1991: 173) is that it is not helpful to set up the debate in such a way that it appears that there can be one answer, one solution, to all questions about the reality of being a man, woman, or otherwise. What is required is a focus upon, and an understanding of, the specific instances that create specific concerns; for example, over which public toilet/bathroom individuals may use, which needs to be balanced with matters of feeling either safe or respected. Paying attention to particular concerns, in particular instances, is likely to be more productive than aiming to provide a universal solution.

A generous reading of de Beauvoir and Irigaray makes it clear that the lives and lived experiences of many women and transgendered individuals demonstrate that the processes for becoming such subjects can be arduous. Thinking and acting differently is not easy. Nevertheless:

> it is better, too, to remain living persons: men and women, than to become neutral, abstract, artificial individuals, members of a social machine which functions more or less efficiently [. . .] and in which identity and relationships between persons come second to the rule of money and to the arbitrary authority of certain decisions. (Irigaray 2000a: 155)

Irigaray's work is contentious, provocative and fruitful. It would have been possible to edit the phrase 'men and women' from this quotation or to replace it with 'persons'. Retaining this phrase is a reminder of the trenchant status of words, ideas and events surrounding questions of 'sex' and 'gender'. What can be taken from Irigaray's account is the need to recognise that language and the world are tied up with what it means to be and live as a person. Such persons have differences that need to be recognised. The danger is that of attempting to iron out difference at the level of language alone, thereby creating a falsely neutral society, submitting ourselves to a societal machine that is concerned not with us but with efficiency. In such a world we are not fully persons; we come second to the rule of money and the arbitrary decisions of others. This sounds like capitalism. It is time to turn to this.

8

Tone, Force and Rhetoric:
Capitalism, Theology and Grammar

In order to reapproach the relation between words and things, one important step, as we have seen, is to recognise that there is a *manner* to how the world unfolds or occurs. Language, as part of the world, also has its manners of expression. Words, phrases and sentences are not inert, they are not presented in a vacuum; they always have a certain quality. Words are spoken loudly, written floridly. As Whitehead puts it: 'No verbal sentence merely enunciates a proposition. It always includes some incitement for the production of an assigned psychological attitude [. . .] This incitement is conveyed partly by the grammatical mood and tense of the verb' (Whitehead 1933: 312).

This chapter will attempt to render Karl Marx's work within the problematic relations of words and things that have been raised in previous chapters. Marx's thought will be presented as sharing with Whitehead, Deleuze, Dewey and Irigaray the view that processes are central to existence, and to thinking, speaking and writing about existence. The reading of Marx offered below will focus on the importance of the 'tone' or 'force' of language. This is not merely a matter of rhetoric. Rather, it points to the need to develop Dewey's emphasis on the manner of existence so that this also applies to the form of language. It is not a question of language being either neutral or biased, describing an objective state of affairs or subjective feelings. These, again, are unnecessary bifurcations. What is required is a recognition of the specific form, the manner, of language. Indeed, this is something advocated by Frege, even as he set out the parameters

135

of analytic philosophy's 'scientific' approach, although this aspect of his thought has not received much attention. For Frege, language statements involve not only sense and reference but also tone and force (see Daly 2013: 87–94). Although Marx does not use such terminology, the extent to which his writing manifests different tones, and certainly a force, is striking: for example in the extensive use of theological terms and concepts to describe the operations of capitalism. Such apparently 'rhetorical' devices, I will argue, are not to be overlooked, as they are an inherent aspect of the argument and point to the complexity of thinking about words and things. As a result, one sub-theme of this chapter is that there is a link between grammar and theology. We have not shed the theological aspect of our words, grammar and thought.

While it may be well known that Nietzsche declared God to be dead, it should be noted that he was not always so optimistic, for example when he stated: 'I fear we did not get rid of God, because we still believe in grammar' (Nietzsche 2004: 17). Just as Derrida traced the 'metaphysico-theological roots' of Western thought and language (Derrida 1976: 13), Nietzsche locates the legacy and role of a Judaeo-Christian God within the structures of language. The model of talking and thinking developed in the West was forged with the same tools that fashioned a specific concept of God. The belief in being, in existence, in the relations between subjects and objects is embroiled in a specific theological outlook. Whitehead makes a related point: 'The secularization of the concept of God's functions in the world is at least as urgent a requisite of thought as is the secularization of other elements in experience' (Whitehead 1978: 207).

It may appear that the modern West has secularised its experience, to a greater or lesser extent. Works of art that were created within an overtly religious milieu, such as Bach's *St Matthew Passion*, are still performed and enjoyed, without having to accede to the tenets or beliefs that they espouse. Whitehead's description of 'the concept of God's functions in the world' is, however, more deep-rooted than this, as will be explained in the following examples of debt and sin and market forces. To reapproach capitalism, and our world, we need to reapproach our language, to secularise it.

God, Market Forces, Debt and Sin

One reason that Martin Luther (1483–1546) objected so strongly to mediaeval Roman Catholicism was the widespread practice of 'plenary indulgences'. These were part of a complex system of forgiveness and absolution that was to be found in the Catholic Church. Plenary indulgences do not absolve sin, but they do 'buy' remission from the consequences of sin, such as physical pain after death in purgatory. The length of time that this pain lasts depends on the seriousness of the sin. Obtaining a plenary indulgence reduces or eliminates this time, this suffering. Originally, these plenary indulgences were envisaged as good works (helping the poor, for example) that were carried out by an individual hoping for a reduction in their punishment after death. However, an 'economic' aspect soon developed in this practice.

In 1343 Pope Clement VI established a 'Treasury of Merit' which encompassed the good works of all Christians of all eras. It was envisaged that the acts of Christ and the saints had established a *surplus* of 'goodness' which could be drawn upon by those in need of redemption. This surplus of goodness constitutes the Treasury of Merit, which was, and still is, under the control of the pope. Through the performance of acts of charity, prayer or fasting, a penitent is able to draw on this Treasury of Merit, thereby gaining redemption and remission from punishment. This theological manoeuvre led to the more general understanding, and practice, of regarding sin as a form of debt, which could therefore be repaid. Money quickly took over from charitable works as the main method of negotiating sinful debt. Giving money to the poor, or a hospital, and later directly to the Church or a priest, became the preferred means by which the debts of sin were paid, and it was the corruption involved in

137

such practices that so incensed Luther. That is to say, it appeared possible to *buy* remission from sin.

The theological and moral legacy of this procedure can still be found in the language and actions surrounding debt, so that debt is seen as 'immoral'; there is a moral obligation for debts to be paid back, to be redeemed. A direct link runs between debt, sin and forgiveness. At its very root, debt retains connotations of sin. The creditor is in the right. The debtor owes more than just money, they are 'indebted' to their creditors. Paying our debts is a moral duty, not just a financial one. Debt makes us penitent, meek, passive. Debt always has a hint of the sinful about it, partly because of the origin of a specific understanding of debt that had its birth in the world of plenary indulgences. We have not rid ourselves of this concept, its practice, its language. We need to secularise debt.

One striking example of this is to be found in the tortuous negotiations and arguments between various Greek governments and the 'Troika' of the Eurozone countries, the European Central Bank and the International Monetary Fund from 2009 onwards. The language in which the argument has been framed is instructive, for example in phrases such as 'debt forgiveness'. It seems that Greece *has* to pay; it would be 'immoral' not to do so. The Greek government must atone for the various economic sins that it has committed over the years. All Greek citizens must take their punishment for their wrongdoings (they need to spend less and work harder, it is claimed).

This moral element has been made even clearer through the counter-claims made by the Greek government. Reaching back into history, some Greek politicians argued that Germany owes Greece reparations for the 'wrongdoing' of the occupation of Greece by the Nazis during the Second World War. Most of such claims for reparation, for the destruction of property, for example, have been rejected out of hand by German politicians. However, there is some sympathy for the Greek government's claim for reparations for the so-called 'occupation loan' (*Besatzungsanleihe*). This was a charge levied by the Nazis on the

Greek government during its occupation of the country from 1942 to 1944. This enforced loan from the Greek government to the occupying Nazi army was supposed to cover the costs incurred by the Nazis during their occupation. The status of this loan is seen by many to be questionable, as it has a different history to the other claims of the Greek government for reparations. Whether this claim is justified or not, the theological aspect remains through an appeal to a moral element: the only way to atone for this original immoral act is through a financial repayment. Once the amounts have been adjusted for inflation, the sin can be erased through an act of plenary indulgence, as money is the sure way to pay both genuine and metaphorical debts. Some might object that such repayments are simply financial. Payments were made between 1942 and 1944 by the Greeks. These should now be repaid by the Germans. It is not, however, the original loan that is the problem. Some loans are forgotten or 'forgiven' after a certain period of time. The reason that this loan is still viable is that it was itself immoral, a sin. Time does not erase sins but money does. The repayment of this loan is not simply financial, a balancing of the economic books. It is a matter of balancing the moral books. Once debts are paid, at either the personal or governmental level, there is a return to a state of balance, to a state of grace, a *forgiving* of debt.

As Max Weber (1864–1920) made clear, the theological element of capitalism is not limited to the relation between sin and debt. He outlined the enduring legacy of a Calvinist conception of predestination on capitalism (for example, through the notion that time should not be wasted; see Weber 2003). A further example can be found in the use that commentators and politicians still make of the well-worn phrase 'the invisible hand', coined by Adam Smith (1723–90), the putative 'father' of modern economics, to refer to the idea that if all individuals pursue their own economic interests, the outcome will be an economy and a society that benefits all of its members. This 'invisible hand' secretly moulds and supports the well-being of all, though it cannot be seen. This is one function of the concept of God, considered as the hidden but beneficent guarantor of humans and their lives. The concept of the 'invisible hand' plays out in the contemporary use of an analogous term, that of 'market forces', which also involves an appeal to an impartial, all-knowing but slightly mysterious mechanism that mimics the action of an unseen, benevolent God. This theological element is bolstered by the advocacy of a 'faith' in economic markets. Unlike belief, faith implies an implicit, unprovable, yet undoubtable truth. Not to have faith in markets is akin to heresy. As will be discussed throughout the remainder of this chapter, it is only possible to understand and analyse capitalism through an appreciation of its theological aspects.

Capitalism and Process

It is important to note that Marx does not treat capitalism as a thing, but as a way of doing things. If capitalism is conceptualised as constituting some kind of a noun that is then picked out by certain words, the problems discussed in Chapters 2 and 3 return with a vengeance. Instead, Marx sets out to delineate the processes inherent in the activities of capitalism.

> Without production, no consumption; but also, without consumption, no production; since production would then be purposeless [. . .] the product, unlike a mere natural object, proves itself to be, *becomes*, a product only through consumption. Only by decomposing the product does consumption give the product the finishing touch. (Marx 1973: 91, emphasis in original)

Traditional models of capitalism may envisage factories, populated by workers and owners, which produce items for consumption by the general population. When products leave the factory gates, they are complete. They exist. Marx disagrees; such items require to be consumed before they can be said to have fully completed their purpose. The product only exists once it is 'decomposed'. The task that Marx sets himself is to explain this very peculiar process.

140

According to Marx, things *become* products. They do so through a process that involves both their production and their consumption. This process always happens in a certain way and is therefore 'adverbial'. Adverbs express the qualities of verbs; they indicate the specific ways in which things are done. Marx's thought can thus be aligned with that of Dewey, Deleuze and Whitehead. It is not just that there are different forms of production (and consumption) in different societies or eras. The differences between these societies and eras lie precisely in their different ways of doing things, of producing and consuming.

> Hunger is hunger, but the hunger gratified by cooked meat eaten with a knife and fork is a different hunger from that which bolts down raw meat with the aid of hand, nail and tooth. Production thus produces not only the object but also the manner of consumption. (Marx 1973: 92)

This is why Marx talks of *modes* of production. Capitalism is only one way, manner or mode of doing things. There have been and will be others.

With regard to the argument being set out in this chapter, what is important is not just the manner (or mode) of capitalism, but the manner of the language that Marx deploys to analyse it. Although capitalism appears to constitute the 'normal' way of doing things, and so permeates our lives and language that it is often taken to be unremarkable, one of Marx's endeavours is to make this apparent normality strange. Indeed, it is so strange that Marx resorts, time and again, to a theological vocabulary. There are two reasons for this. First, the peculiarity of capitalism requires a theological approach to understand its mysteriousness. Second, and relatedly, Marx insists that capitalism is not a thing but a way of doing things. This entails that it cannot be countered or critiqued simply by indicating its status. This is no simple, quasi-scientific task of isolating an object in order to manipulate or change it. That capitalism is a manner of being, involving adverbial processes, means that a recognition of its manners and qualities is required to understand and critique it. Language is a

141

key resource for this. Marx's deployment of theological concepts and quotations is not mere rhetoric or hyperbole, but an integral part of his argument.

From Commodities to Theology[1]

One question that Marx sets himself to answer is 'How does money make more money?' It is often taken for granted that the economy should grow, year on year. Monthly, quarterly and yearly growth figures are keenly anticipated. Underlying such assumptions is the belief that money 'grows', can multiply itself. Marx's analysis of this belief, and the manoeuvres that give rise to it, takes up most of the 900 or so pages of the first of the three volumes of his monumental book *Capital*. His initial assertion is that money, left to itself, will not grow. If £100 is left under a mattress for a year it will still be £100; it will not have magically turned into £105. To understand how money grows, we need to follow its adventures in the world. A crucial part of such adventures is the transformation of money into the things of the world, into commodities. Marx, therefore starts his analysis with a discussion of the role and status of a commodity.

> A commodity appears at first sight an extremely obvious, trivial thing. But its analysis brings out that it is a very strange thing, abounding in metaphysical subtleties and theological niceties. (Marx 1990: 163)

The modern world is populated (and littered) with a vast array of commodities: mobile phones, holidays, cups of coffee. Not

---

1. Walter Benjamin (2004) also made a study of some of the connections between religion, theology, capitalism and Marxism. He believed that capitalism is a 'cultic religion'. He also argues that Marxism (as opposed to Marx) has a tendency to become theological, and that this is not a good thing. While I do not wholly disagree with Benjamin, I have not addressed his arguments in any detail as I believe that I am dealing with a different set of concerns.

only are such commodities often taken for granted, but so are the processes that enable them to surround us. Marx argues that commodities are not as simple as they seem. Unpicking them will reveal 'metaphysical subtleties' and 'theological niceties'. Our ignorance of, and lack of interest in, the real processes that go to make up commodities means that the way we talk and think of them is superficial and inadequate. Our thought and language have not caught up with the world, with the peculiar world of commodities. To invoke and explain these mysterious commodities, Marx uses what he considers to be the only appropriate language available – the theological.

According to Marx, the processes of capitalism involve the exchange of commodities, the establishment of complex sets of relations between things. It should be noted that Marx does not start his quest by analysing money or financial exchange. His interest is in what makes such exchange possible; what is it in a commodity that makes it exchangeable with other commodities? As will be seen shortly, money (or the money-relation) does not explain the character of commodities but itself needs to be explained.

Marx's analysis of the commodity starts by making a distinction between 'use-value' and 'exchange-value'. Use-value indicates the usefulness of an item; a table can be used to place things on, a chair to sit on, etc. Exchange-value is more complex but is, according to Marx, crucial. If commodities only confronted each other in terms of their use-value, it would not be possible to evaluate their interrelations, or to exchange them. For example, how can the usefulness of a chair, considered as something to sit on, be compared with the usefulness of a table, considered as something to place things on? 'It is overlooked that the magnitudes of different things only become comparable in quantitative terms when they have been reduced to the same unit' (Marx 1990: 140–1).

In order to make different items exchangeable, it is necessary to move beyond their immediate uses and to assign them a different kind of value, one that reduces them 'to the same unit'.

This is the role of exchange-value, which asserts an equivalence between two things that at first sight seem resolutely different. A commodity 'appears as the twofold thing it really is as soon as its value possesses its own particular form of manifestation, which is distinct from its natural form. This form of manifestation is exchange-value' (Marx 1990: 152). Marx insists that due attention be paid to this step of making things equivalent. It might appear banal but, in a sense, it is an act of violence. All the differences of the world, as apparently expressed in the vast array of things in the world (wheat, coffee, holidays, healthcare, mobile phones, etc.) have been forced into a strategic equivalence, their differences denied or ignored, so that they are reduced to 'mere commodities', as potentials for being exchanged.

The examples that Marx uses in his discussion are linen and a coat.[2]

> Whether 20 yards of linen = 1 coat or = 20 coats or = x coats, i.e. whether a given quantity of linen is worth a few coats or many coats, it is always implied, whatever the proportion, that the linen and the coat, as magnitudes of value, are expressions of the same unit, things of the same nature. Linen = coat is the basis of the equation. (Marx 1990: 141)

Coats and linen are only 'of the same nature', are only equal, in a very specific sense, that of its 'value-form': 'the linen acquires a value-form different from its natural form' (Marx 1990: 143). The form of exchange-value is different from the 'natural' form of a commodity (its use-value). Exchange-value is a matter of enforced equality (which has some resonance with Irigaray's comments on the forcing of a neutral society). This makes it possible for linen, for example, to be thought of, and treated, as equivalent to something else, to another commodity (for example, a coat). For Marx, it is the commodity *form*, it is value-*form* that are the keys to capitalism (not commodities and value, as many commentators and economists think). Pre-echoing the

---

2. One reason for this is because linen can be made into coats.

insights of Dewey and Whitehead, Marx asserts that form, in the sense of 'quality' or 'manner', is an integral aspect of the existence of commodities, is not an addition. Commodities and value are, in themselves, relational. This implies not that there is an objective base, some primary substance, some 'thing' that is named by the words 'the economy', which it is possible to know (as both traditional and even many Marxist economists seem to think). Rather, there are relations that are always presented in a certain way. There is no noun-like entity 'out there' in the world, there is only the manner of the presentation, which is itself a necessary element of the presentation.

In order to make his point, Marx introduces a theological element: '[The linen's] existence as value is manifested in its equality with the coat, just as the sheep-like nature of the Christian is shown in his resemblance to the Lamb of God' (Marx 1990: 143). The specific form, or nature, of a Christian (as opposed to that of other humans) is expressed in the characteristic of being 'sheep-like'; a characteristic that is shared by Christ, when he is described as 'the Lamb of God'. It is this characteristic that enables these two radically different things (humans and God) to be compared. It is important not to underestimate the strangeness of making an equivalence between certain humans (Christians) and God. Likewise, the strangeness of making all commodities equivalent, in that they can all be exchanged for each other, should not be underestimated. The equivalence of commodities is, in this sense, a concept of the same status as those of theology.

Having set out the complexity of the way in which we envisage things as equivalent, Marx moves on to how these things are actually exchanged. Once more, he resorts to theological imagery: 'A born leveller and cynic, it [a commodity] is always ready to exchange not only soul, but body, with each and every other commodity' (Marx 1990: 179). The commodity is always dual, as it has a use-value and an exchange-value. To explain this, and to make this duality understandable, Marx decides that the best, if not the only, route is via the terms 'body' and 'soul'. Its body is the use-value of a commodity; its exchange-value is its soul, in that it expresses the 'form of appearance of its own value' (Marx 1990: 179). This soul is, however, promiscuous, as the commodity is prepared to trade with any and all other commodities: 'the linen recognizes in it [the coat] a splendid kindred soul' (Marx 1990: 143). The form, the manner of exchange-value is not merely 'like' or akin to the soul. It *is* the soul of the commodity.

The examples provided so far may be suggestive, but it could perhaps be countered that they are more to do with questions of imagery, style or even rhetoric, than cornerstones of Marx's conceptual analysis. One aim of this chapter is to argue that such matters of style are more than 'mere rhetoric' and are integral to the *form* of argument. The discussion so far has dealt only with the possibility of exchange and has not analysed the role and status of money in this. As will be seen in the next section, it is when money enters the scene that theological language becomes fully necessary to express the bizarre processes inherent in capitalism.

'The Love of Money . . . '

Marx has traced the *apparent* equivalence of all commodities but has not described how they are actually exchanged under capitalism. That which makes it possible to move from an *apparent* equivalence to a real equivalence is an intermediary system against which all commodities can be judged. This system is money. Marx is not talking about the ability of gold and silver coins to buy goods. He is talking of money as a widespread system, one that holds throughout a society and so appears universal. This is the form of money that appears in modern capitalism (apparently guaranteed by the state or a national bank). Money is what enables us to compare a cup of coffee (£2) with a holiday (£730). Going without a daily coffee would make savings equivalent to a holiday over the course of a year. Anything can be compared to anything. More than that, anything can be turned into anything through the mediation of money. Houses can be turned into cars and holidays, pianos and vases, and so on. This is where the notion of the apparent equality of all items, reducing them to a common denominator that allows *any* thing to be exchanged for any other thing, further displays its violence. The specificity of existence, in the things of the world, is ignored and flattened to a sparse realm of utter exchangeability, of capitalism. This includes not just things, but persons.

When Marx introduces money as this 'universal equivalent', he does so by quoting, in Latin, two lines from the Book of Revelation of the New Testament. It is only in the footnote that this is translated, including the line 'no man [*sic*] might buy or sell, save that he had the mark, or the name of the beast, or the number of his name' (cited in Marx 1990: 181). It is not so much that money is evil, or a tool of the antichrist, but it is 'supernatural', in that it relies upon a universal equivalence that operates beyond the remit and capacity of any individual, and yet to which all individuals must submit themselves. Moreover:

> In order, therefore, that a commodity may in practice operate effectively as exchange-value, it must divest itself of its natural physical body and become transformed from merely imaginary into real gold, although this act of *transubstantiation*[3] may be more 'troublesome' for it than the transition from necessity to freedom for the Hegelian 'concept', the casting of his shell for a lobster, of the putting-off of the old Adam for Saint Jerome. (Marx 1990: 197, emphasis added)

Leaving aside the reference to Saint Jerome, it is the concept of transubstantiation that is of interest. To grasp what Marx means by 'transubstantiation', it is necessary to delve briefly into scholastic philosophy. In this school of thought, existence could be separated into two aspects: 'essences' and 'accidents'. Essence constituted the core of the existence of a specific thing, making it what it 'is'. This is to be contrasted with the accidents

---

3. This is not Marx's only mention of transubstantiation. He uses the term again in a later discussion (Marx 1990: 203).

of such things. Accidents make up the temporary properties or characteristics that a thing exhibits to humans. This is similar, but not identical, to the distinction between primary and secondary qualities discussed in Chapter 3. The key element of this distinction is that essence remains the same while accidents can change. Wax has an essence that endures even if its accidents change, for example, if it warms up and changes from being solid to being liquid; 'underneath' (in essence) it is still just wax.

In Catholic theology, this distinction between accident and essence has been used to explain what happens when the bread and wine presented at the altar during a Mass are purportedly transformed into the body and blood of Christ. As opposed to most Protestants, who view this as a symbolic exercise, Catholics see it as a genuine transformation. The bread really turns into flesh, the wine really turns into blood. The reason such changes are not seen is because, as distinct from the usual course of events, the *accidents* stay the same but the *essence* changes. The *essence* of the bread has changed into Christ's body, the essence of the wine into his blood. However, the accidents, and appearance, have remained those of bread and wine.

This, according to Marx, is what happens during the exchange of a commodity into money. As discussed earlier, commodities need not only to be produced but to be consumed. The mediating element of this process is exchange. In the process of exchange the commodity might appear to stay the same (as do its accidents), but its essence changes. It becomes money. It is easy to overlook this alteration, as the commodity appears still to have the same form. It is just that this commodity is now owned by someone else. Likewise, the money still has the same outward appearance (accidents), it is just that it is now owned by someone else. Marx insists that to fully understand the process through which the use-value of the commodity has been transformed into money, it is necessary to recognise it as transubstantiation. This is no metaphor or rhetorical device, it is simply the most accurate way of conceptualising the strange metamorphosis that is at the heart of capitalism, namely, commodity exchange.

There is, indeed, a double transubstantiation: that of the commodity into money and the money into a commodity, which is not usually recognised, since, again, the accidents of both remain the same even though their essences have changed. To understand the manner of capitalism, there is a need to elucidate the 'whole mystery of commodities, all the magic and necromancy that surrounds the products of labour on the basis of commodity production' (Marx 1990: 169). If a coat is sold for £10, and is exchanged for a £10 note, it might seem that the same coat and the same £10 note appear after the exchange; it is just that the coat and the £10 are now in different places. However, to fully understand the process, it is necessary to realise that the coat has transubstantiated, and so has the money.

As is the case with the commodity, the money used to facilitate the exchange of commodities is involved in a complex set of relations, as the exchange of commodities involves movement, process, circulation.

> Circulation becomes the great social retort into which everything is thrown, to come out again as the money crystal. Nothing is immune from this alchemy, the bones of the saints cannot withstand it. (Marx 1990: 229)

Money is now a 'money crystal' which comes into being as part of the enormous flow of commodities. Circulation operates like the device in a laboratory or factory (a retort), which heats up whatever is thrown into in, melts it, and spews it out, re-formed. This process is akin to alchemy, in which lead is turned into gold. It is also similar to Marx's use of the term transubstantiation. There is more than a hint of the dark arts, as 'the bones of the saints cannot withstand' the white heat of the process of circulation.

One outcome of Marx's setting of commodities and money in terms of relations and processes is that, like capitalism, money should not be treated as a thing, as having the status of a noun. It is more accurate to talk of the 'money-relation' rather than 'money':

149

every trace of the money-relation disappears in the money-names pound, thaler, franc, ducat, etc. The confusion caused by attributing a hidden meaning to these cabalistic signs is made even greater by the fact that these money-names express both the values of commodities and, simultaneously, aliquot parts of a certain weight of metal. (Marx 1990: 195)

The 'money-names' such as dollar, pound, euro or yuan do not represent or capture what is going on in the production and exchange of commodities. Instead they are 'cabalistic signs' that express simultaneously the thing that is being exchanged and their own worth, supposedly. At this point, Marx is assuming that the various currencies are tied to a fixed, external standard – namely, the gold standard. This may not be the case in most modern Western economies, but currencies are still treated as if they have a genuine value, even if this is only to be judged by the rate at which a currency can be exchanged for another currency. Indeed, this makes Marx's point even more salient, as the value of a currency is only ever relative to the value of other currencies, which are relative to others, and so on. There is no ground or foundation. Their values are chimerical.

There are numerous other occasions when Marx dips into theological or religious phrases. Near the beginning of his famous discussion of the 'fetishism of the commodity and its secret', he writes: 'In order, therefore, to find an analogy we must take flight into the misty realm of religion' (Marx 1990: 165). Later, he mentions how 'linen [. . .] *goes the way of all flesh*, enters the chrysalis state as gold, and thereby simultaneously completes the first metamorphosis of a third commodity' (Marx 1990: 207, emphasis added). Again, Marx believes it is only possible to understand the transformation of money into commodities and vice versa through a religious reference. Also: 'Modern society [. . .] greets gold as its Holy Grail, as the glittering incarnation of its innermost principle of life' (Marx 1990: 230). He also cites the start of Psalm 42: 'As the hart pants after fresh water, so pants his soul after money' (Marx 1990: 236). These are not mere allusions or rhetorical devices. In order to explain the operations of money, its mysterious, almost miraculous character, there is a requirement to resort to the language of theology to adequately describe the peculiarities and specificities of capitalism. This is not to suggest that Marx either believes in the concepts of theology or the existence of a deity. Following Nietzsche and Whitehead, Marx recognises that the theological permeates our language and our thought in ways that need to be recognised and brought to the fore. Once this is done, the task of 'the secularization of the function of the concept of God', as Whitehead puts it, can be taken up.

Conclusion

While many may be critical of capitalism, they are wary of the alternatives and ask questions such as: 'Capitalism may not be perfect, but what other option do we have?' The implication of such a question is that the end of capitalism would be apocalyptic. It would mean the dissolution of our institutions and ways of life, leading to civil war. The images invoked are similar to those used to describe the end of days when the Four Horsemen of the Apocalypse come to wreak their vengeance; images that are drawn from Christian theology. The onus thus falls on the non-believer in capitalism to justify their desire to bring an end to the world, by bringing an end to capitalism. One way of doing this is by developing a faith in the future, seeing socialism or communism as the salvation that is yet to come.[4] This is the reverse of the previous position, and can be viewed as just as extreme. Having laid out two 'apocalyptic' alternatives, the collapse of capitalism or communism, the current muddled state of affairs is able to continue.

Philippe Pignarre and Isabelle Stengers (2011: 23–30) have stressed that rather than take one side in this argument, we should

---

4. This is related to Walter Benjamin's claim that a range of 'messianic' elements can be identified throughout history (see Benjamin 2005).

refuse to be put in any kind of 'either/or' situation. To challenge or critique capitalism is often seen as naïve. One reason for this is that the options are always presented in terms of either/or questions, which themselves suggest irreconcilable bifurcations. We have to accept austerity *or* we will face bankruptcy; we must control immigration *or* we will be overrun; and so on. Pignarre and Stengers call these 'infernal alternatives'. The power of these questions comes from the way they are set up, from their grammatical structure. Nietzsche and Whitehead would counsel that care is taken when the world is presented, via language and grammar, as constituted by a gulf between two utterly antagonistic propositions. The task is to refuse to accept the basis of an either/or proposition: '*Either* you are for greater police powers *or* you will have accept more terrorist attacks.'

Such a refusal does not entail advocating some tepid middle ground or third way. When faced with an apparent split or gulf between two opposing positions, it is not helpful to try and reconcile them. What is required is an analysis of that which grants energy to the problem that itself produced such a split or bifurcation. In this way, it is possible to reapproach and move beyond the problem. 'A clash of doctrines is not a disaster – it is an opportunity' (Whitehead 1932: 230). This applies to the apparent either/or dilemmas of capitalism. As Pignarre and Stengers put it, the task is that of 'naming it [capitalism] in a way that allows its type of power to be encountered; its mode of influence [. . .] to be deciphered' (Pignarre and Stengers 2011: 30).

This chapter has discussed some of the problems involved in naming capitalism, in using nouns to pick out the complex manner of existence which we call 'capitalism'. This involves paying attention to the language of capitalism itself, and the kind of language needed to describe its processes. Our world is very peculiar, and capitalism has a major role in its peculiarity, so much so that it can be 'named' as theological. This is not a solution to the problem; there is probably no one solution. Whatever moves are made need to be aware of the strange imbrications of capitalism, language and the world, and not to be shy of using theological concepts and language to reorient our understanding and critique.

9

Conclusion

'Philosophy begins in wonder. And, at the end, when philosophic thought has done its best, the wonder remains' (Whitehead 1938: 232). This book has focused on the relation between language and the world, not in order to provide answers or a scheme that is to be learned and applied, but in an attempt to reinvigorate our thoughts and appreciation of both language and the world. Words and the world can be both wonderful and terrible. The predominance in contemporary academic thought of strains of both analytic philosophy (which attempts to demystify language) and semiology (with its emphasis on the determining role of external structures) risks diluting the 'wonder' of both language and the world. The questions and arguments set out in the previous chapters have attempted to reinstate some of the imagination and speculation that Whitehead views as essential both to philosophy and to the world.

Yet, as I have argued elsewhere (Halewood 2018), speculation should be treated with caution. Recent moves to reinsert speculation into philosophy and social theory may be welcomed, but should be treated with restraint. As mentioned in Chapter 1, Whitehead insists that 'Speculative boldness must be balanced by complete humility before logic, and before fact. It is a disease of philosophy when it is neither bold nor humble, but merely a reflection of the temperamental presuppositions of exceptional personalities' (Whitehead 1978: 17). Philosophy and robust thinking require a specific form of speculation, which Whitehead describes as 'imaginative generalization' (Whitehead

1978: 5). This mention of 'generalization' is important as it distinguishes philosophical speculation from idle speculation about who may or may not be the next president or prime minister, or financial speculation on the stock market. Speculation, for Whitehead, involves moving beyond the concerns and problems of a specific field to a wider field of thought. This freedom of thought, however, must be balanced by a humility in the face of both logic and fact. This balance is to be tested by assessing the appropriateness of the generalisations developed with their applicability in other areas, and with respect to other problems. 'The success of the imaginative experiment is always to be tested by the applicability of its results beyond the restricted locus from which it originated' (Whitehead 1978: 5).

While previous chapters have not been presented in terms of speculation, they have asked for a level of imagination, a shifting of perspective, with regard to questions about the relation of language and the world. In doing so, ideas and evidence from the fields of philosophy, social theory, feminism, anthropology and literature have been offered. 'The chief danger to philosophy is narrowness in the selection of evidence' (Whitehead 1978: 337). If philosophy and social theory are to thrive they need to be alive to the concerns of the world, and of those entities that populate the world, including humans. The danger of academic specialisation is that it leads its proponents down interesting but narrow avenues of thought and writing. This is not merely a matter of making academic work 'more relevant' or 'accessible to the public', it is a question of the very status of philosophy, and the relevance of academic thinking.

'Philosophy destroys its usefulness when it indulges in brilliant feats of explaining away [. . .] Its ultimate appeal is to the general consciousness of what in practice we experience' (Whitehead 1978: 17). The remit of philosophy is not given in advance. The version of philosophy inherited in the West sometimes makes it appear that certain specific concerns are central: wisdom and truth (Plato); the mind, rationality and knowledge (Descartes); avoiding the pitfalls of language (Wittgenstein). This is, of course, a very particular, and perhaps personal, selection. Its purpose is to point to the specificity of our philosophical heritage and to remind us that we cannot know in advance what will constitute a genuine philosophical problem, or what directions philosophy might take. However, this is not to advocate a multiplication of the application of already formed ideas and formulae in either philosophy or sociology to a wider range of 'topics', such as the philosophy of artificial intelligence, the sociology of the body, the philosophy of love, the sociology of food. Rather, there is a need for an openness to that which Whitehead calls 'the general consciousness of what in practice we experience'. 'A new idea introduces a new alternative; and we are not less indebted to a thinker when we adopt the alternative which he [sic] discarded. Philosophy never reverts to its old position after the shock of a great philosopher' (Whitehead 1978: 11). Whitehead lists Plato, Aristotle, Thomas Aquinas, Descartes, Spinoza, Leibniz, Locke, Berkeley, Hume, Kant and Hegel as examples of such 'great philosophers'. What is more important is the notion of 'shock' and the fact that philosophy itself is changed by its impact. It is not possible to sketch in advance what shock might affect philosophy, and where this might come from.

It is important, at this point, to return to Whitehead's notion of 'humility'. I am certainly not claiming that this book should provide any such shock. The ideas and analyses set out in previous chapters are an attempt to be more open to the kinds of shock that writers such as Whitehead, Deleuze, Dewey and Irigaray offer. This involves a reorientation of our position in relation to language and the world. It might also ask for a reconsideration of our concern with 'reality'.

In Chapter 1, the problematic of words and things was set out with reference to the question of correlationism as discussed within Speculative Realism. The problem of correlationism is a very specific one. As should be clear by now, my intention was not to provide any simple solutions, taking the word 'solution' in its literal sense of dissolving. This would be more a case of explaining away. We do not need a better concept of reality. This is one of my concerns with Speculative Realism. Some of the thinkers involved in this project seem to believe that it is possible to discover the definitive explanation of 'reality'. Yet if they ever did make such a discovery, they would have thought themselves out of business.

This is another reason why 'the concept of reality' is so dangerous. It is a concept that is both tantalising and powerful, but it leads us to try and subsume so many different things under the same conceptual umbrella. This is not to suggest that the problem of 'reality' can be sidestepped through some clever analysis, or by deconstructing our concept of reality, or by simply saying 'world' instead. We can accept the critical force of the problem of correlationism as set out by Speculative Realism without accepting that this is the only problem, the most immediate one, and that what is required is a better, more complete concept of reality. Trying to account for the manner of existence of *every* thing in the universe, in existence, is to remain within an old-fashioned notion of 'reality'. To return, tentatively, to the chemical metaphor of 'solutions', perhaps philosophy is more like a catalyst. It enables change, and I hope that some elements of some of the chapters in this book have offered some small changes.

With a final nod towards Whitehead's notion of humility, it is worth concluding by placing language and humans within their respective limits. Both are important, and worthy of consideration and thoughtful analysis, but neither are ultimates. For, as Whitehead puts it: 'Language is incomplete and fragmentary, and merely registers a stage in the average advance beyond ape-mentality' (Whitehead 1933: 291).

Bibliography

Ansell-Pearson, K. (1999), *Germinal Life. The Difference and Repetition of Deleuze*, London: Routledge.

Austin, J. L. (1975), *How to Do Things With Words*, Oxford: Clarendon Press.

Ayer, A. J. (1971), *Language, Truth and Logic*, Harmondsworth: Penguin.

Badiou, A. (2009), *Logics of Worlds. Being and Event 2*, trans. Alberto Toscano, London: Continuum.

Barthes, R. (2000), *Mythologies*, London: Vintage.

Beauvoir, de. S. (1949), *Le deuxième sexe I. Les faits et les mythes*, Paris: Gallimard.

Beauvoir, de. S. (1949), *Le deuxième sexe II. L'expérience vécue*, Paris: Gallimard.

Beauvoir, de. S. (1988 [1953]), *The Second Sex*, London: Picador.

Benjamin, W. (2004), 'Capitalism as Religion', in *Walter Benjamin. Selected Writings Volume 1. 1913–26*, Cambridge, MA: Harvard University Press, pp. 288–90.

Benjamin, W. (2005), 'On the Concept of History', in *Walter Benjamin. Selected Writings Volume 4. 1938–40*, Cambridge, MA: Harvard University Press, pp. 389–408.

Berkeley, G. (1996), *Philosophical Works: Including the Works on Vision*, ed. Michael Ayers, London: J. M. Dent.

Brown, R. (1968 [1958]), *Words and Things. An Introduction to Language*, Toronto: Free Press.

Bryant, L. (2015), 'Correlationism', in P. Gratton and P. J. Ennis (eds), *The Meillassoux Dictionary*, Edinburgh: Edinburgh University Press, pp. 46–8.

Carnap, R. (1959), 'The Elimination of Metaphysics through Logical Analysis of Language', in A. J. Ayer (ed.), *Logical Positivism*, Glencoe, IL: The Free Press, pp. 60–81.

Charlton, W. (2014), *Metaphysics and Grammar*, London: Bloomsbury.

Daly, C. (2013), *Philosophy of Language. An Introduction*, London: Bloomsbury.

Debaise, D. (2006), *Un empirisme spéculative. Lecture de Procès et réalité de Whitehead*, Pris: Vrin.

Debaise, D. (ed.) (2011), *Philosophie des Possession*, Paris: Les Presses du Réel.

Debaise, D. (2017), *Nature as Event. The Lure of the Possible*, Durham, NC: Duke University Press.

Deleuze, G. (1988), *Foucault*, Minneapolis: University of Minnesota Press.

Deleuze, G. (1990), *The Logic of Sense*, London: Athlone Press.

Deleuze, G. (1993), *The Fold. Leibniz and the Baroque*, London: Athlone Press.

Deleuze, G. (1994), *Difference and Repetition*, London: Athlone Press.

Deleuze, G., and Guattari, F. (1994), *What is Philosophy?*, London: Verso.

Derrida, J. (1976), *Of Grammatology*, Baltimore: Johns Hopkins University Press.

Dewey, J. (1958 [1925]), *Experience and Nature*, rev. 2nd edn of 1929, New York: Dover Publications.

Dewey, J. (2005 [1934]), *Art as Experience*, New York: Perigee.

Doxiadis, A., and Papadimitriou, C. H. (2009), *Logicomix. An Epic Search for Truth*, London: Bloomsbury.

Dreyfus, H., and Rabinow, P. (1982), *Michel Foucault. Beyond Structuralism and Hermeneutics*, Hemel Hempstead: Harvester Press.

Durkheim, E. (2008 [1915]), *The Elementary Forms of the Religious Life*, Mineola, NY: Dover Publications.

Faber, R., and Goffey, A. (2014), *The Allure of Things. Process and Object in Contemporary Philosophy*, London: Bloomsbury.

Ford, Lewis. S. (1984), *The Emergence of Whitehead's Metaphysics 1925–1929*, Albany: State University of New York Press.

Foucault, M. (1967), *Madness and Civilization*, London: Tavistock.

Foucault, M. (1970), *The Order of Things*, London: Tavistock.

Foucault, M. (1972), *The Archaeology of Knowledge*, London: Routledge.

Foucault, M. (1976), *The Birth of the Clinic*, London: Routledge.

Foucault, M. (1980), *Power/Knowledge. Selected Interviews and Other Writings 1972–1977*, ed. G. Colin, Hemel Hempstead: Harvester Press.

Foucault, M. (1982), 'The Subject and Power', in H. Dreyfus and P. Rabinow (eds), *Michel Foucault. Beyond Structuralism and Hermeneutics*, Hemel Hempstead: Harvester Press, pp. 208–26.

Foucault, M. (1984 [1976]), *The History of Sexuality. Volume One*, Harmondsworth: Penguin.

Foucault, M. (1991 [1975]), *Discipline and Punish. The Birth of the Prison*, Harmondsworth: Penguin.

Fowler, H. W. (1937 [1926]), *A Dictionary of Modern English Usage*, Oxford: Clarendon Press.

Fraser, M. (2006), 'Event', *Theory, Culture and Society*, 23.2–3: 129–32.

Frege, G. (1980), *Translations from the Philosophical Writings of Gottlob Frege*, ed. Peter Geach and Max Black, Oxford: Blackwell.

Giddens, A. (1984), *The Constitution of Society: Outline of the Theory of Structuration*, Cambridge: Polity Press.

Gratton, P., and Ennis, P. J. (eds) (2015), *The Meillassoux Dictionary*, Edinburgh: Edinburgh University Press.

Halewood, M. (2010), 'Badiou, Whitehead and the Politics of Metaphysics', in R. Faber, H. Krips and D. Pettus (eds), *Event and Decision*, Newcastle: Cambridge Scholars Press, pp. 170–91.

Halewood, M. (2011a), *A. N. Whitehead and Social Theory. Tracing a Culture of Thought*, London: Anthem Press.

BIBLIOGRAPHY

Halewood, M. (2011b), 'John Dewey sur la Possession: l'expérience, la co-appartenance et la philosophie adverbiale', in D. Debaise (ed.), *Philosophies de Possession*, Paris: Les Presses du Réel, pp. 71–106.

Halewood, M. (2012), 'On Natural-Social Commodities. The Form and Value of Things', *British Journal of Sociology*, 63.3: 430–50.

Halewood, M. (2014), *Rethinking the Social through Durkheim, Marx, Weber and Whitehead*, London: Anthem Press.

Halewood, M. (2017), 'Situated Speculation as a Constraint on Thought', in A. Wilkie, M. Rosengarten and M. Savransky (eds), *Speculative Research. The Lure of Possible Futures*, London: Routledge, pp. 52–64.

Halewood, M. (2018), 'A Question of Faith? Stengers and Whitehead on Causation and Conformation', *Substance*, 47.1: 80–95.

Hall, S. (1982), 'The West and the Rest', in S. Hall and B. Gieben (eds), *Formations of Modernity*, Cambridge: Polity Press, pp. 276–80.

Haraway, D. (1991), *Simians, Cyborgs, and Women. The Reinvention of Nature*, London: Free Association Books.

Harman, G. (2009), *Prince of Networks. Bruno Latour and Metaphysics*, Melbourne: re.press.

Harrison, B. (1979), *An Introduction to the Philosophy of Language*, London: Macmillan.

Heidegger, M. (1971), *Poetry, Language, Thought*, New York: Harper and Row.

Homer, S. (2005), *Jacques Lacan*, London: Routledge.

Irigaray, L. (1985a), *Speculum of the Other Woman*, Ithaca: Cornell University Press.

Irigaray, L. (1985b), *This Sex Which Is Not One*, Ithaca: Cornell University Press.

Irigaray, L. (1993), *je, tu, nous. Toward a Culture of Difference*, London: Routledge.

Irigaray, L. (1994), *Thinking the Difference. For a Peaceful Revolution*, London: Athlone Press.

Irigaray, L. (1996), *I Love to You. Sketch for a Felicity Within History*, London: Routledge.

Irigaray, L. (2000a), *Democracy Begins Between Two*, London: Athlone Press.

Irigaray, L. (2000b), *To be Two*, London: Athlone Press.

Kohn, E. (2013), *How Forests Think. Toward an Anthropology Beyond the Human*, Berkeley: University of California Press.

Lacan, J. (1977), *Écrits. A Selection*, London: Tavistock.

Latour, B. (1993), *We Have Never Been Modern*, Hemel Hempstead: Harvester Wheatsheaf.

Latour, B. (1999), *Pandora's Hope: Essays the Reality of Science Studies*, Cambridge, MA: Harvard University Press.

Latour, B. (2005), *Re-assembling the Social. An Introduction to Actor-Network-Theory*, Oxford: Oxford University Press.

Lévi-Strauss, C. (1994), *The Raw and the Cooked*, London: Pimlico.

Levitin, D. (2006), *This is Your Brain on Music. Understanding a Human Obsession*, London: Atlantic Books.

Locke, J. (1997 [1690]), *An Essay Concerning Human Understanding*, Harmondsworth: Penguin.

Lycan, W. G. (2000), *Philosophy of Language. A Contemporary Introduction*, London: Routledge.

Marsh, D. (2014), *For Who the Bell Tolls. The Essential and Entertaining Guide to Grammar*, London: Guardian Books and Faber and Faber.

Marvell, A. (1985), 'The Garden', in H. Gardiner (ed.), *The Metaphysical Poets*, Harmondsworth: Penguin, pp. 255–8.

Marx, K. (1973), *Grundrisse. Foundations of the Critique of Political Economy*, Harmondsworth: Penguin.

Marx, K. (1990), *Capital. Volume 1*, Harmondsworth: Penguin.

Marx, K., and Engels, F. (1986), *Collected Works. Volume 28*, London: Lawrence and Wishart.

Marx, K., and Engels, F. (1987), *Collected Works. Volume 29*, London: Lawrence and Wishart.

Marx, K., and Engels, F. (1996), *Collected Works. Volume 35. Capital Volume 1*, London: Lawrence and Wishart.

Mead, M. (1949), *Male and Female: A Study of the Sexes in a Changing World*, London: Victor Gollancz.

Meillassoux, Q. (2008), *After Finitude. An Essay on the Necessity of Contingency*, London: Continuum.

Miller, A. (2007), *Philosophy of Language*, London: Routledge.

Nietzsche, F. (2004), *The Twilight of the Idols and The Antichrist*, Mineola, NY: Dover Publications.

Peirce, C. S. (1958), *Selected Writings*, New York: Dover Publications.

Pignarre, P., and Stengers, I. (2011), *Capitalist Sorcery. Breaking the Spell*, Basingstoke: Palgrave Macmillan.

Plato (2014), 'Cratylus', in *The Dialogues of Plato. Volume Two*, ed. B. Jowett, Good Time Classic Book Collection, pp. 62–183.

Russell, B. (1905), 'On Denoting', *Mind*, 14.56: 479–93

Samson, C. (2003), *A Way of Life that Does not Exist: Canada and the Extinguishment of the Innu*, London: Verso.

Saussure, F. de (1983), *Course in General Linguistics*, London: Duckworth Press.

Sayer, D. (1987), *The Violence of Abstraction. The Analytic Foundations of Historical Materialism*, Oxford: Blackwell.

Searle, J. (1970), *Speech Acts*, London: Cambridge University Press.

Shaviro, S. (2009), *Without Criteria: Kant, Whitehead, Deleuze, and Aesthetics*, Cambridge, MA: MIT Press.

Shaviro, S. (2014), *The Universe of Things. On Speculative Realism*, Minneapolis: University of Minnesota Press.

Spender, D. (1980), *Man Made Language*, London: Routledge and Kegan Paul.

Stengers, I. (2010), *Cosmopolitics. Volume 1*, Minneapolis: University of Minnesota Press.

Stengers, I. (2011), *Thinking With Whitehead. A Free and Wild Creation of Concepts*, Cambridge, MA: Harvard University Press.

Stengers, I. (2014), 'Speculative Philosophy and the Art of Dramatization', in R. Faber and A. Goffey (eds), *The Allure of Things. Process and Object in Contemporary Philosophy*, London: Bloomsbury, pp. 188–217.

Stevens, W. (1984), *Collected Poems*, London: Faber and Faber.

Stone, A. (2006), *Luce Irigaray and the Philosophy of Sexual Difference*, Cambridge: Cambridge University Press.

Stones, R. (2005), *Structuration Theory*, Basingstoke: Palgrave Macmillan.

Stryker, S., and Whittle, S. (eds) (2006), *The Transgender Studies Reader*, London: Routledge.

Weber, M. (2003 [1904–05]), *The Protestant Ethic and the Spirit of Capitalism*, Mineola, NY: Dover Publications.

Weiner, J. (2004), *Frege Explained*, Chicago and La Salle: Open Court.

White, M. (1997), *Isaac Newton: The Last Sorcerer*, London: Fourth Estate.

Whitehead, A. N. (1919), *An Enquiry Concerning the Principles of Natural Knowledge*, London: Cambridge University Press.

Whitehead, A. N. (1927a), *Symbolism. Its Meaning and Effect*, New York: Macmillan.

Whitehead, A. N. (1927b), *Religion in the Making*, Cambridge: Cambridge University Press.

Whitehead, A. N. (1932 [1925]), *Science and the Modern World*, Cambridge: Cambridge University Press.

Whitehead, A. N. (1933), *Adventures of Ideas*, Cambridge: Cambridge University Press.

Whitehead, A. N. (1938), *Modes of Thought*, Cambridge: Cambridge University Press.

Whitehead, A. N. (1964 [1920]), *The Concept of Nature*, Cambridge: Cambridge University Press.

Whitehead, A. N. (1978 [1929]), *Process and Reality. An Essay in Cosmology* (Gifford Lectures of 1927–28), ed. D. Griffin and D. Sherburne, New York: The Free Press.

Whitford, M. (1991), *The Irigaray Reader*, Oxford: Blackwell.

Whittle, S. (2006), 'Foreword', in S. Stryker and S. Whittle (eds), *The Transgender Studies Reader*, London: Routledge, pp. xi–xv.

Williams, J. (2016), *A Process Philosophy of Signs*, Edinburgh: Edinburgh University Press.

Wittgenstein, L. (1974 [1921]), *Tractatus Logico-Philosophicus*, London: Routledge and Kegan Paul.

Wittgenstein, L. (1988 [1953]), *Philosophical Investigations*, Oxford: Blackwell.

Index

After Finitude (Meillassoux), 2
Ansell-Pearson, Keith, 60
Aristotle, 38–9, 67, 90
  on primary substance, 38, 48

Beauvoir, Simone de, 112–17
  on asymmetry of 'masculine' and
    'feminine', 114–15
being, manner of, 69–70, 135
Bergson, Henri, 52
bifurcation, 11, 47, 59, 66, 69, 90, 95,
    97–8, 108, 113, 123, 132, 135,
    152
  of actualities, 45
  as inconsistent, 46
  of nature, 34, 44–8, 49, 68, 87, 88
  not a one-off event, 45–6
  and 'sex'/gender, 126
  and structure-agency debate, 59–62
Bryant, Levi, 2–3

Capital (Marx), 145
Carnap, Rudolf, 25, 26
commodities, 143–7
  soul of, 145–6
Concept of Nature, The (Whitehead), 45
contrast(s), Deleuze on, 59–60
correlationism, 2–3, 10–11, 37, 100,
    156–7

dark energy, 46
dark matter, 46
Debaise, Didier, 11
Deleuze, Gilles, 51–70, 98–9
  attitude toward language and the
    world, 69

on Foucault, 59–61
on infinitive form of verbs, 53–7
language as part of potentiality of
  existence, 54–6
language as part of the world, 54–5,
  62
on the limitations of 'reality', 55–6,
  57–8
on predication, 62–3
on present form of verbs, 53,
  57–63
on sense as constructed, 64–7, 85
on speculation, 5
on statements, 60
Derrida, Jacques, 90, 103
Descartes, René, 92–3, 155
Dewey, John, 8, 71–88, 119
  against secondary qualities, 78
  on co-belonging, 79–80
  on meaning, 83, 85
  on the natural and the social, 81–3
  on nature, 73, 77–80
  on nature as incomplete, 80
  on portability, 84–5
  on reason, 81
  on the supernatural, 8, 81
Dictionary of Modern English Usage, A
  (Fowler), 111, 120
Difference and Repetition (Deleuze), 98
Discipline and Punish (Foucault), 82
Durkheim, Emile, 8–9

*Essay Concerning Human Understanding,
  An* (Locke), 40
essence and accidents (scholastic distinction between), 148–9

event(s), 52, 75, 91
  and adverbs, 77–8
  communication of events, 54–5
  and experience, 79, 86
  language, events and limitation, 57
  language, events and the present,
    60–2
  language as event, 54
  make language possible, 53, 55
  relationship between language and
    events, 56
  and sense, 63–7
  and 'sex' and gender, 134
eventful character of existence, 51, 74,
  81, 87
  and adverbs, 88
exchange-value and use-value, 143–5
experience, 74–7
  and adverbs, 76
  located *in* the world, 75

Foucault, Michel, 59–61, 82–3
  power as 'how' things are done, 83
Fowler, H. W., 111–12, 120
Frege, Gottlob, 17–21, 31–2, 85, 136
  importance of (mathematical) logic
    for language, 17–19
  language prioritised over the world,
    19–20
  on predicates as incomplete, 19
  on proper names, 17–18
  on true and false, 20–1

gender and language, 111–12
Giddens, Anthony, 59
grammar
  as prescriptive or descriptive, 126–30
  and theology, 136
Guardian, The, 120

Haraway, Donna, 130, 133
Harman, Graham, 7, 11
Heraclitus, 52
History of Sexuality, Volume One, The
  (Foucault), 82
Hume, David, 92–3

Irigaray, Luce, 116–19, 121–6, 128,
  131–4
  on grammar as limiting thinking,
    116–17

on language and bodies, 122–4
on need for specific female subjectivity, 121, 125–6
on possession, 118–19
on subsumption of female into
  male, 123–4
on 'withoutness' of body, 124–5

James, William, 51

Kant, Immanuel, 2–3
Kohn, Eduardo, 104–9
  limits to his notion of semiosis,
    107–9
  links semiosis and life, 108–9

Lacan, Jacques, 32, 58
Levitin, Daniel, 43–4, 77
  music as a 'secondary quality', 43
linguistic determinism, 4–5
linguistic relativity, 4–5
linguistic turn, 1
Locke, John, 40–2, 44–6
Logic of Sense, The (Deleuze), 53, 55
Luther, Martin, 137

McAloon, Paddy, viii
Man with the Blue Guitar, The (Stevens),
  68
market forces and theology, 139–40
Marsh, David, 120
Marvell, Andrew, 49
Marx, Karl, 52, 135–51
  on capitalism as process, 140–1
  on commodities, 142–6
  on enforced equality of exchange,
    144–5
  on exchange-value and use-value,
    143–5
  importance of 'form' for, 145
  relation to adverbs, 141
  theological language, 141–2,
    145–51
  on transubstantiation, 147–9
*Mathematical Principles of Natural
  Knowledge* (Newton), 40
Meillassoux, Quentin, 2–3, 6–7, 11,
  37, 38, 100
money, 146–7, 149–51
  money relations, 149–50

Newton, Isaac, 40–1, 43
Nietzsche, Friedrich, 136

Peirce, C. S., 105–9
  on icons, 106
  on indices, 106–7
  on signs, 107
Pignarre, Philippe, 151–2
Plato, 155
plenary indulgences, 137–8
possession, 72–4, 79–80, 86–7
  compared with Greek thought, 72
  threefold character of, 72–3
prepositions, 75, 86–8
primary and secondary qualities, Locke
  on, 41–3, 84–5
Process and Reality (Whitehead), 12, 45,
  51, 77, 93, 95, 96
propositions
  Deleuze on, 63–4
  as thought content of sentence, 20

'reality', concept of, 7–9, 11, 156–7
'reality', problem of, 6–9, 156–7
rhetoric, 135–6
Russell, Bertrand, 21–4, 31–2
  on descriptions, 22–4
  on existential and universal quanti-
    fier, 22–3
  and logical analysis of language,
    22–4
  unfavourable attitude to metaphys-
    ics, 24

Sapir-Whorf hypothesis, 4–6, 7
Saussure, Ferdinand de, 27–30, 31–2,
  85
  both signifier and signified as
    arbitrary, 29
  distinction between signifier and
    signified, 28–30
  not concerned with truth or
    falsehood, 30
Second Sex, The (de Beauvoir), 112
secondary qualities, 41–3, 78
'sex'/gender distinction, 110–11
  and events, 134
  problems with, 112–13
sin and debt, 138–40
Smith, Adam, 139

speculation, 10, 12, 55, 154–5
speculative realism, 1–2, 6
Spinoza, Baruch, 52
Stengers, Isabelle, 12, 151–2
  on 'infernal alternatives', 152
Stevens, Wallace, 68
Stones, Rob, 59
structure-agency debate, 58–9, 61–3
symbolic reference, 107–8
  in Whitehead, 91, 96, 99–102,
    103–4
Symbolism: Its Meaning and Effect
  (Whitehead), 95

things
  and Bruno Latour, 35
  difference between 'things' and
    'objects', 35–7
  as open concept, 34–5
This Sex Which Is Not One (Irigaray),
  125
Through the Looking Glass (Lewis
  Carroll), 58
Tichý, Jindra, 115–16
Toscano, Alberto, 1
Tractatus Logico-Philosophicus (Wittgenstein), 24–5
transgender, 111, 132, 133
transubstantiation, 147–9
treasury of merit, 137

Vienna Circle, 25–7

Weber, Max, 139
Whitehead, Alfred North
  on bifurcation, 12, 44–8
  on bodilyness, 90–1, 94–5
  on the body, 90–1
  on causal efficacy, 93–5, 97–8
  on difficulty of word 'and', 1
  on duality of perception, 91–4, 96
  on eye-strain and eye-efficacy, 97–9
  on 'gulfs', 5
  on humility, 156, 157
  on imaginative generalisation,
    155–6
  particular version of realism, 103
  on presentational immediacy, 93–5
  on primary substance, 37–40
  on propositions, 26

reluctance to use word 'reality', 12
on secularisation of concept of God,
    136
on speculation, 12, 155
on speculative boldness, 10
on speculative physics, 47
on subject and object as relative
    terms, 60

on subject-predicate axis, 37–8
on symbolism, 99–103
on 'things', 35
on 'withness' (of the body), 89–90,
    95–7
on the word 'and', 1
Williams, James, 102
Wittgenstein, Ludwig, 24–7, 155

EU representative:
Easy Access System Europe
Mustamäe tee 50, 10621 Tallinn, Estonia
Gpsr.requests@easproject.com

www.ingramcontent.com/pod-product-compliance
Lightning Source LLC
Chambersburg PA
CBHW071027280326
41935CB00011B/1486